D0827756

INSIGHT ⊙ GUIDES

NEW YORK

POCKET GUIDE

◎ Walking Eye App

YOUR FREE EBOOK AVAILABLE THROUGH THE WALKING EYE APP

Your guide now includes a free eBook to your chosen destination,
for the same great price as before. Simply download the Walking Eye
App from the App Store or Google Play to access your free eBook.

HOW THE WALKING EYE APP WORKS

Through the Walking Eye App, you can purchase a range of eBooks and destination
content. However, when you buy this book, you can download the corresponding
eBook for free. Just see below in the grey panel where to find your free content and
then scan the QR code at the bottom of this page.

Destinations: Download essential destination
content featuring recommended sights and
attractions, restaurants, hotels and an A–Z of
practical information, all available for purchase.

Ships: Interested in ship reviews? Find independent reviews of river and ocean ships in this
section, all available for purchase.

eBooks: You can download your free accompanying digital version of this guide here. You
will also find a whole range of other eBooks,
all available for purchase.

Free access to travel-related blog articles
about different destinations, updated on a
daily basis.

HOW THE EBOOKS WORK

The eBooks are provided in EPUB file format. Please note that you will need an eBook reader installed on your device to open the file. Many devices come with this as standard, but you may still need to install one manually from Google Play.

The eBook content is identical to the content in the printed guide.

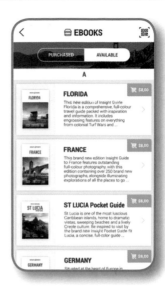

HOW TO DOWNLOAD THE WALKING EYE APP

1. Download the Walking Eye App from the App Store or Google Play.
2. Open the app and select the scanning function from the main menu.
3. Scan the QR code on this page – you will then be asked a security question to verify ownership of the book.
4. Once this has been verified, you will see your eBook in the purchased ebook section, where you will be able to download it.

Other destination apps and eBooks are available for purchase separately or are free with the purchase of the Insight Guide book.

TOP 10 ATTRACTIONS

BROOKLYN BRIDGE
Stroll across this 19th-century icon. See page 32.

THE GUGGENHEIM
As well known for its architecture as for its paintings. See page 54.

STATUE OF LIBERTY
Welcoming millions to New York since its dedication in 1886. See page 28.

MOMA
Home to one of the world's best collections of modern art. See page 42.

TIMES SQUARE
Get up close to the spectacle of this iconic world landmark. See page 34.

EMPIRE STATE BUILDING
The famed skyscraper offers eye-popping views of Manhattan. See page 47.

AMERICAN MUSEUM OF NATURAL HISTORY
From dinosaurs to planets, it's all here. See page 63.

GREENWICH VILLAGE
A laid-back feel characterizes the infamously bohemian 'Village'. See page 74.

THE METROPOLITAN MUSEUM OF ART
A vast and fabulous trove of historical treasures. See page 51.

CENTRAL PARK
Unwind in New York's playground. See page 56.

A PERFECT DAY

9.00am

Breakfast

Enjoy the quintessential breakfast of New Yorkers – bagel, lox, and cream cheese – at Katz's Delicatessen on the Lower East Side. After breakfast stroll down Ludlow where you can window-shop the hip neighborhood's boutiques.

10.15am

Lower East Side origins

Just a couple of doors down from Delancey on Orchard Street is the Lower East Side Tenement Museum. Here you can step back in time and learn about the immigrants who originally populated the Lower East Side with a visit to the tenement building built in 1863.

11.15am

Walk to Brooklyn

Continue heading south, through Chinatown, to the Brooklyn Bridge entrance at the end of Centre Street. Cross the bridge via the walkway to arrive in Brooklyn at the other side of the East River.

12.30pm

Pizza perfect

A Brooklyn institution, Grimaldi's Pizzeria (1 Front Street; exit the bridge via the first stairs) is a must. After lunch, wander along Water Street. Grab a hot chocolate from Jacques Torres before heading to the promenade along the East River in Brooklyn Bridge Park. The views of lower Manhattan are picture-perfect.

IN **NEW YORK**

5.30pm

Central Park
After the Frick, take a walk through Central Park, which is just across Fifth Avenue. There is an entrance two blocks north at 72nd and Fifth Avenue. Stroll to the Lake, Strawberry Fields, or the Shakespeare Garden.

8.00pm

Broadway
Hit the Great White Way and enjoy one of the many Broadway or off-Broadway performances.

2.30pm

Old Masters in the afternoon
Take the subway to the Upper East Side. The Frick Collection (1 East 70th Street) is a wonderful, intimate museum, much more manageable than the nearby Met. Built in 1913, the mansion of Henry Frick was designed to accommodate his growing collection of works by artists including Rembrandt, El Greco, Vermeer, and Gainsborough.

10.30pm

City lights
Top off your day with a perfect panoramic view of the city with all its sparkling lights from Top of the Rock on the 69th floor of the Rockefeller Center.

CONTENTS

INTRODUCTION

First-time visitors to New York usually come with wide eyes and high expectations. The quintessential urban landscape, the Big Apple does not disappoint. No matter what it is you are after, you will find it: great theater, marvelous museums, luxurious hotels, fascinating history, exciting nightlife, sumptuous dining. Peace and quiet can even be found, in the rooms of high-rise hotels far above the teeming streets, or by venturing into the upper reaches of Central Park, or walking out onto the terrace overlooking the Hudson River at the Cloisters.

At first, New York can be a little overwhelming however, once you get over the crowded streets and the wailing sirens, you can start to see that there is more to New York than its tourist attractions and museums. It is a place where people live.

☉ THE 9/11 EFFECT

Every American over a certain age can tell you the story of where they were and what they were doing when President John Kennedy was assassinated on November 22, 1963. Now, every New Yorker can tell you where they were and what they were doing the morning of September 11, 2001 when two terrorist-hijacked planes hit the World Trade Center. The average New Yorker has emerged from the tragedy of September 11 feeling no less rushed and impatient about day-to-day life, but certainly less invincible and far more vulnerable. A visit to the National September 11 Memorial & Museum on the site of the former Ground Zero and the Freedom Tower is a must for visitors who wish to pay their respects in person.

A CITY TRANSFORMED

If anything characterizes New York today, it is how much the city has raised itself up from the darker days of the 1970s and 1980s. Crime has now dropped to levels New Yorkers had not seen since the early 1960s, and the city is generally clean and efficient. As a result, both tourists and business people flock here in ever-increasing record numbers every year (61.8 million visitors in 2017).

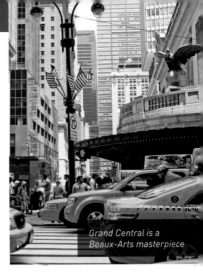

Grand Central is a Beaux-Arts masterpiece

If you want to see an example of how the city can reinvent itself, just look at Times Square. Until the early 1990s, the 'square' was filled with pornographic theaters, adult bookstores, and abandoned buildings. The Port Authority bus terminal was filled with hustlers and touts, and 42nd Street was really not a place one wanted to be after dark. Today Times Square is still choked, but with new, high-profile office buildings and hotels, refurbished Broadway theaters, shiny entertainment complexes, and tens of thousands of tourists. The adult theaters and bookstores have been banished for the most part, and media giants like MTV have reclaimed the space along with well-attended attractions including Madame Tussaud's Wax Museum.

Not that the story is uniformly positive. The New York area has some of the highest unemployment and poverty rates in the country. The disparity between the rich and the poor is greater than ever. Most of the new housing being built in the

The French-inspired Bryant Park

city will be affordable only to those with the highest incomes. Nevertheless, almost every New York neighborhood has a good story to tell.

A GORGEOUS MOSAIC

It is difficult for mere mortals to live in such a complicated, crowded, and expensive city, so people can easily lose their tempers. But, for a place as large and diverse as New York City undoubtedly is, everyone gets along pretty well. The five boroughs – Manhattan, Brooklyn, Queens, the Bronx, and Staten Island – have a total population of around 8.5 million. Brooklyn is the most populous, and Brooklyn and Queens each have more residents than Manhattan. There are more Italians than in Venice, more Irish than in Dublin, and more Jews than in Jerusalem.

As a hub for immigration since colonial days, New York has always welcomed the world. Today people still arrive in large numbers, searching for wealth, happiness, freedom, or just a job, making the mixture even richer.

By the end of their first trip to New York, most visitors are hooked. Nothing is quite as exhilarating as walking the crowded streets of Midtown for the first time, or encountering works of art you've only read about in books, or seeing the Statue of Liberty looming over you from the ferry dock; or even just strolling through Central Park on a blustery winter afternoon.

A BRIEF HISTORY

In 1524 Giovanni da Verrazano, a Florentine in the service of France, discovered what is now called New York Harbor. However, it would be a hundred years before the first settlers came to the area. Today the entrance to the harbor (the Verrazano Narrows) and the bridge across it are named after him.

NEW AMSTERDAM

Excitement finally began to build over the region's possibilities in 1609, after the Englishman Henry Hudson, working for the Dutch East India Company, sailed up what is now the Hudson River to Albany. In 1624, the new Dutch West India Company sent the first settlers to what is now Lower Manhattan. The following spring the colonists built a small town at the site, calling it New Amsterdam. The first two Dutch governors of the territory, Peter Minuit and Peter Stuyvesant, oversaw the development of a lively trading post. According to a popular city creation myth, it was Peter Minuit who in 1626 purchased the entire island of Manhattan from Native Americans for the equivalent of $24 in beads and cloth, at the site of present-day Bowling Green.

From the beginning, New Amsterdam was the most cosmopolitan center in the New World. The earliest immigrants included Walloons, Scandinavians, Germans, Spaniards, and Portuguese Jews, not to mention black slaves from the Caribbean. In 1643 a priest counted 18 languages spoken in this town of 1,500 inhabitants. An atmosphere of religious tolerance even attracted British dissidents from New England.

In 1653 Governor Peter Stuyvesant built a wall across the expanse of the island (at present-day Wall Street) in an effort to protect the Dutch settlers from the British, who had settled

Map of New Amsterdam from 1660

much of the area around New Amsterdam. But the effort was unnecessary. Unable or unwilling to put up a fight, the Dutch settlers surrendered to an English fleet on September 8, 1664. King Charles II gave the colony to his brother, the Duke of York, and New Amsterdam was re-christened New York.

NEW YORK

Although the city again came under Dutch control in 1673 (again without a fight) and was briefly known as New Orange, a treaty the following year returned it to British control. In the 18th century the town grew into a city of 25,000 and life became more comfortable. A city hall and several churches were built, and New York saw the foundation of King's College (today's Columbia University) as well as the creation of its first newspaper. Little of this era remains today. St. Paul's Chapel, built in 1766, is the oldest remaining church in New York. The Morris-Jumel mansion in Harlem also dates from this time.

British control of the colony of New York was a mixed success. Anti-British sentiment started early. In 1735 John Peter Zenger, publisher of the anti-government *New-York Weekly Journal*, was acquitted on charges of slander, an early victory for freedom of the press. (You can read more about the history of this victory at Federal Hall National Memorial in Lower Manhattan.) The city was split between loyalists to the crown and pro-independence 'patriots.' On June 27, 1775, half the town went to cheer George Washington as he left to take command of the Continental Army in Boston, while the other half were down at the harbor giving a rousing welcome to the English governor, who had just returned from London. Similarly, the New York delegates voted against an early version of the Declaration of Independence.

THE NEW REPUBLIC

New York remained a British stronghold throughout the Revolutionary War and only gave up after the final surrender in Virginia in 1781. Two years later England recognized the independence of the American colonies. Washington returned triumphantly to New York and bade farewell to his officers at Fraunces Tavern. He later became the country's first president, when the city was briefly the first capital of the new United States of America. Washington took the oath of office on the balcony of the original Federal Hall (formerly the New York City Hall), then went to pray at St. Paul's Chapel, where you can see his pew.

Although Philadelphia took over as the nation's political capital in 1790, New York remained America's commercial center. In 1800 (the same year Alexander Hamilton built the Grange, which is in today's Harlem), the population had reached 60,000–twice what it had been ten years earlier.

The city was soon beset with housing shortages and sanitation problems. In the heat of summer, when disease and epidemics were commonplace, the inhabitants would escape to their 'country' homes in such far-flung places as the village of Greenwich (now Greenwich Village) or the wilderness that became today's Upper East Side. In 1811 the state legislature came to the conclusion that any further growth of New York City must be regulated. The Randel Commission proposed that all new streets should only cross each other at right angles, with streets running east–west

Cemetery to park

Many of New York's parks were originally potter's fields, where indigent people were buried. Both Washington Square Park and Bryant Park started out with this function.

and avenues north–south. (Broadway was exempted.) The plan was immediately adopted, and as a result, everything above 14th Street is now a grid.

BURGEONING TOWN

When the Erie Canal opened in 1825, linking the Great Lakes to the Hudson River, New York became the ocean gateway for an immense hinterland. Business flourished and shipyards abounded in this major port. However, housing was still substandard and most residents lived in crowded conditions. In December 1835 a fire destroyed the heart of the business district around Hanover and Pearl streets, including almost all that remained from the Dutch era. But the city recovered quickly from this calamity.

In 1853 the Crystal Palace of the first American World's Fair went up in present-day Bryant Park. That same year, the state legislature authorized the building of a great public space, Central Park; the architects, Calvert Vaux and Frederick Law Olmsted, were chosen five years later, the same year the Crystal Palace was destroyed by fire.

By 1860, the city's population had reached an unruly 800,000. Governing the city proved difficult, riots occasionally erupted, and crime was becoming a big problem. Rampant government corruption was also taking its toll. William Marcy Tweed ran New York City along with his cohorts in the Tammany Hall political organization. He managed to fleece the city of some $200 million. When 'Boss Tweed' was finally arrested in 1871, the city was in bad shape indeed.

New York nevertheless once again proved its resilience and bounced back. The late 19th century and early 20th witnessed the city's most dramatic growth to date. Many of New York's existing magnificent buildings were built at this time. New York banks financed the construction of the railways that opened up the western lands, the expansion of mines and mills, and the development of the new petroleum and automobile industries. Huge fortunes were made by the Vanderbilts, Rockefellers, Morgans, Carnegies, and Fricks, among others. These tycoons amassed fabulous art collections and funded many of the philanthropic and cultural institutions that make New York what it is today, from the Metropolitan Museum and Metropolitan Opera to the Frick Collection and the Rockefeller Center.

MASS IMMIGRATION

During the second half of the 19th century influxes of immigrants crowded into New York in search of a new and better life. The potato famine in Ireland and revolutionary ferment in Central Europe brought the Irish and Germans, who were soon followed by Italians, Poles, and Hungarians. The first important wave of Jews fleeing the pogroms of Russia and Eastern Europe arrived in the 1880s. Over 2 million newcomers landed in the city between 1885 and

Late 19th-century immigrants

The 9/11 Memorial

1895, welcomed (after 1886) by the Statue of Liberty.

While the middle class moved to west-side neighborhoods near Central Park, the comfortable brownstone houses and mansions of the rich spread up Fifth Avenue and onto the east side. In 1870, construction started on a bridge to connect New York City with Brooklyn, a sizeable city in its own right. The invention of the elevator by Elisha Otis made it possible to construct 'skyscrapers' up to the amazing height of eight or ten stories.

In 1898, New York City (from then on known as Manhattan), Queens, Brooklyn, the Bronx, and Staten Island merged to form Greater New York, with a population of more than 3 million. After London, Greater New York was the world's most populous city.

The early years of the 20th century witnessed further impressive growth. Genuine skyscrapers – including the Flatiron Building (1902) – were built, the first subway line opened (1904), and Manhattan and Brooklyn were linked by an under-river subway tunnel (1908). When the business boom finally burst in 1929, bread lines and jobless people became a common sight; a shantytown even sprang up in Central Park. In 1934 a dynamic Italian-born mayor named Fiorello La Guardia fought to introduce an important number of public-welfare measures and civic reform initiatives, which have characterized the city ever since.

HIGHS AND LOWS

After World War II, the United Nations set up its headquarters in New York on the banks of the East River, on land donated by the Rockefeller family. The 1950s saw phenomenal growth in the city but also economic downturn. New highways and cheaper cars and houses encouraged city-dwellers to move out to the suburbs.

⊘ SKYSCRAPERS

By the early 20th century, the development of 'steel skeleton' construction had finally made it possible to build tall. The first genuine skyscraper in New York was the **Flatiron Building**, erected in 1902 and with 22 stories. The **Equitable Building**, however, which appeared on Lower Broadway in 1916, was a 40-floor monster on an 'H'-shaped ground plan that filled an entire block. The walls were perpendicular, without any tiering, which plunged the whole neighborhood into shadow. The city was compelled to pass a 'zoning law,' which stipulated that the upper floors of a skyscraper should be tiered to allow light through to the streets below. This resulted in the so-called 'wedding-cake' style of building, examples of which include the **Chrysler** and **Empire State Buildings** (1930 and 1931). Designed by Mies van der Rohe with Philip Johnson, and completed in 1958, the **Seagram Building** on Park Avenue was a simple tower with a straight facade, following the rules of the International Style. It overcame the zoning law by having a plaza at its base, setting the trend for later developments such as the Rockefeller Center.

Such a concentration of very tall buildings could never have been built without sturdy foundations, and the billion-year-old gneiss bedrock of Manhattan is as solid as it gets. Its closeness to the surface makes for relatively easy construction.

At the same time, in part because of this retreat, portions of the inner city began to decline. Even the beloved Brooklyn Dodgers moved to Los Angeles in 1958. True, Lincoln Center was built in the 1960s, and the World's Fair was held in Flushing Meadows, Queens, in 1964–65, but racial tensions also led to riots in Harlem, Bedford-Stuyvesant, and the South Bronx. The city reached a low point in 1975 when New York teetered on the edge of bankruptcy.

After mixed fortunes in the 1980s, when the city was known for its high crime rate, the 1990s brought better times. Things started looking up during the mayoralty of David Dinkins, the city's first black mayor, elected in 1989. But most of the improvements were not seen until the arrival of Rudolph Giuliani in 1993. A Republican mayor in a decidedly Democratic city, he brought order to the streets. After September 11, 2001, he took on the unexpected role as the public face of a city in turmoil. Mayor Michael Bloomberg, owner of the financial media empire that bears his name, succeeded him in January 2002. Over his three terms, Bloomberg launched public health initiatives (smoking and trans-fat bans), expanded bike lanes, and helped the city weather storms both literal (Hurricane Sandy) and figurative (the 2008 financial crisis).

New Yorkers continue to display their resilience in the face of repeated threats, adapting as necessary and getting on with their lives. The 9/11 Memorial opened 10 years after the devastation at Ground Zero with the connected museum opening in 2014.

In the same year, Bill de Blasio replaced Bloomberg as mayor, having run on a populist platform with an interest in addressing the economic inequality in the city. He also launched New York City's Identification Card Program, with the aim of facilitating access to city services for illegal immigrants and the homeless. De Blasio was sworn in for a second term on January 1, 2018 having won re-election with 66.5 percent of votes against Republican Nicole Malliotakis in November 2017.

HISTORICAL LANDMARKS

1609 Englishman Henry Hudson is the first European to step on to the island known to the local Algonquin Indians as Mannahatta.

1624 The Dutch West India Company establishes a settlement on the southern tip of Mannahatta, calling it New Amsterdam.

1664 War between England and Holland. New Amsterdam surrenders and is renamed New York after the Duke of York.

1776 The Revolutionary War begins; the colonies declare independence. British troops occupy New York until 1783.

1785–90 New York is capital of the new United States of America.

1830 Irish and German immigrants begin arriving in great numbers.

1835 Part of Manhattan is ravaged by the 'Great Fire.'

1861–5 American Civil War. Draft riots in Five Points neighborhood.

1865 Italians, Jews, and Chinese begin arriving in large numbers.

1886 Statue of Liberty, a gift from France, is unveiled.

1892 Ellis Island becomes the entry point for immigrants.

1929 The Wall Street Crash, and the start of the Great Depression.

1933–45 Europeans take refuge in New York from Nazi persecution.

1941 The US enters World War II.

1973 The World Trade Center opens.

1990 David Dinkins becomes the city's first African-American mayor.

1993 Rudolph Giuliani voted in as mayor and gels 'tough on crime.'

2001 Terrorists crash two hijacked planes into the World Trade Center. The buildings collapse, killing close to 3,000 people.

2008 Wall Street finds itself at the center of the global financial crisis.

2011 9/11 Memorial opens. Occupy Wall Street protesters descend on Lower Manhattan.

2014 Democrat Bill de Blasio is elected mayor of New York.

2015 One World Trade Center opens its Observatory for tourists.

2017 Queens native Donald Trump is inaugurated as the 45th President of the United States of America.

2018 De Blasio is sworn in as Mayor of New York City for the second term. Cortlandt Street subway station reopens after 17 years.

Fall in the West Village

WHERE TO GO

While the majority of visitors to New York never leave Manhattan, there is more to the city than its most famous borough. Those who venture to Brooklyn, for example, will find a world-class art museum along with parks, gardens, and fascinating ethnic neighborhoods. One of the country's great zoos is located in the Bronx, near an equally notable attraction, the New York Botanical Garden. In Queens you will find a top-notch filmmaking museum. Meanwhile, the journey to Staten Island is that borough's highlight, a ferry ride right by the Statue of Liberty, and best of all, it is free.

However, Manhattan is the focus of most visitors' attentions, with its wealth of sights and activities. Only 13.5 miles (22km) long and 2 miles (3.5km) wide, New York's most popular borough is what everyone calls 'the city.' Getting your bearings in this metropolis is remarkably easy thanks to the grid system. Apart from Lower Manhattan – where the thoroughfares twist, turn, and usually have names instead of numbers – all roads running from west to east are called 'streets' and those running from north to south are called 'avenues.' Streets are numbered from south to north and avenues from east to west. Some avenues also have names, such as York Avenue, Lexington Avenue, Park Avenue and Madison Avenue (street signs and addresses list Sixth Avenue as Avenue of the Americas, but New Yorkers rarely call it that). Inclusion of 'West' (W) or 'East' (E) in addresses shows whether it lies west or east of Fifth Avenue. There is just one avenue that doesn't conform to this pattern: Broadway cuts across the island diagonally.

DOWNTOWN

In Lower Manhattan, at the island's southern tip, is the oldest, most historic part of the city; the Financial District corre-
sponds roughly to the area south of Worth Street, which begins
just below Chinatown. Here you'll find Wall Street, One World
Trade Center, the 9/11 Memorial, South Street Seaport, and
ferries to Staten Island and the Statue of Liberty. After years of
neglect, clubs and bars have moved in, making the area worth
a visit even after 7pm. A good source of information on developments in Lower Manhattan is the Alliance for Downtown
New York, Inc. at www.downtownny.com.

ONE WORLD TRADE CENTER AND 9/11 MEMORIAL

For decades, the most visible tourist attraction in Lower
Manhattan was the World Trade Center. It was a huge complex of offices, a hotel, shopping malls, subway stations and
the twin towers themselves. When the towers were opened in
1970, they were the tallest buildings in the world.

⊙ ICON OF HOPE

Remarkable as it might seem, a huge globe-shaped metal
sculpture survived the tons of metal and concrete that
crashed down upon it on 9/11. The *Sphere* by Fritz Koenig
had stood for more than 30 years in the World Trade Center
Plaza. In March 2002, it was moved to nearby Battery Park,
where, on the first anniversary of the attack, an eternal flame
was lit in memory of the victims. In 2017 the sculpture was
returned to the World Trade Center where it will reside per-
manently in Liberty Park.

After September 11, 2001 – when the towers became the target of the country's worst terrorist attack – the construction site where the complex once stood became a moving memorial. The former Ground Zero now holds as much, if not more meaning for visitors, as when they came to marvel at the buildings themselves. Today, the shimmering **One World Trade Center ❶** (formerly known as Freedom Tower) rises up at the

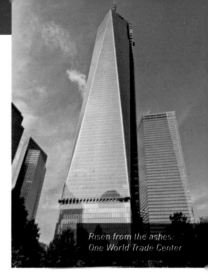

Risen from the ashes: One World Trade Center

center of the site, and the surrounding **9/11 Memorial** offers a tranquil place to reflect and honor the victims.

Completed in 2014 to a design by David M. Childs, One World Trade Center is the highest building in the Western Hemisphere, standing 1,776ft (541 meter) high. Its observation deck (https://oneworldobservatory.com; daily Jan 4–April 30 and Sept 5–Dec 20 9am–9pm, May–Sept 4 8am–9pm, Dec 21–Jan 3 8am–8pm) on the 102nd floor offers unrivalled views over the city. Access is provided thanks to a $4 billion transportation hub connecting subway, train, ferry, and bus lines in a striking structure designed by acclaimed Spanish architect Santiago Calatrava. Also connected to the transportation hub is the Cortlandt Street subway station which, after suffering severe damage in the September 11, 2001 terrorist attack, reopened in 2018.

The memorial, which incorporates the footprints of the twin towers into its design, was dedicated on the 10th anniversary

Castle Clinton

of the attack. Visitors to the memorial and its accompanying museum need to reserve a pass, which is free, from www.911memorial.org.

BATTERY PARK CITY

When the World Trade Center was being built in the late 1960s, some 30 million tons of excavated landfill were dumped on adjoining Hudson River docks to create the site of what became, in the 1980s, **Battery Park City**, a collection of high- and low-rise apartment and office buildings and parks. A lovely esplanade lined with parks and gardens stretches along the river from Stuyvesant High School on the north end, all the way south to historic Battery Park.

The highlight of the **World Financial Center** is the fine **Winter Garden**, a public atrium ringed by shops, restaurants, and bars. Grab take-out from a café and join the stockbrokers on one of the benches, or enjoy a more upscale lunch at one of the sit-down restaurants.

A stroll down the promenade is a pleasant way to spend an hour, and also a great place to view the sunset. At the end of the promenade, near Bowling Green subway station, is the **Museum of Jewish Heritage** ❷ (www.mjhnyc.org; Sun–Tue 10am–6pm, Wed–Thu 10am–8pm, Fri 10am–5pm, until 3pm on Fri early Nov–mid-Mar, closed Sat and Jewish holidays). Beyond the first floor's interesting multimedia introductory show are galleries about Jewish life and culture; the second floor is devoted to the Holocaust, while the third floor contains exhibits about Judaism today. By focusing on the complexity of Jewish life in the 20th century, the museum give a less harrowing account than others devoted solely to the Holocaust.

Nearby is **Battery Park**, a leafy expanse at the tip of Manhattan. Most visitors head for **Castle Clinton**. Originally the West Battery – a fortification to help protect ships in New York from the English navy – the building dates to 1811. By 1824 its military mission was fulfilled and the fort became a concert hall, immigration checkpoint, and even for a while, the New York City Aquarium. The National Park Service took over the building in the 1940s and renamed it Castle Clinton. It was re-opened in 1975 as a small museum and as the ticket office for ferries to the Statue of Liberty and Ellis Island (see page 28).

⊙ LIBERTY SCIENCE CENTER

From the docks outside the World Financial Center, you can take the New York Waterway Ferry to Colgate Ferry Terminal (Paulus Hook) in New Jersey (www.nywaterway.com; every 7–8 minutes on weekdays) to connect to the Hudson-Bergen Light Rail (Essex Street Station to Liberty State Park Station; www.njtransit.com) for the **Liberty Science Center** (www.lsc.org; daily 9am–5.30pm). Though not technically a New York City attraction, it is nevertheless a fun place to explore. The exhibitions are designed to appeal to all ages and include a skyscraper area, where visitors can walk along a beam above the exhibition floor and see beams recovered from the World Trade Center. The center also includes an IMAX theater.

Across from Battery Park's northern tip, at the foot of Broadway, is a small triangular patch called **Bowling Green**. It is said that this is where in 1626, Peter Minuit bought Manhattan from Native Americans for the equivalent of $24. Today it is the site of one of New York's many Greenmarkets, selling fresh local produce (Tue and Thu 8am–5pm).

Looming over the square is the **Old Customs House**, which is now the home of the **National Museum of the American Indian** ❸ (www.nmai.si.edu; daily 10am–5pm, Thu until 8pm), a branch of the Smithsonian Institution in Washington, DC. The museum celebrates Native American culture and showcases a variety of artifacts. The other Smithsonian branch in NYC is the Cooper-Hewitt, reopened after renovation on the Upper East Side.

Staten Island Ferry

If you are on a tight budget, a ride on the free Staten Island Ferry is a great way to get a closer look at the Statue of Liberty. There is little of interest to visitors on Staten Island, but the 20-minute ferry ride is well worth the trip. Catch the ferry from the southern tip of Battery Park and you'll get stunning views of the Statue of Liberty and the Manhattan skyline, and since the ferry runs 24 hours a day, you can get the same view at night.

STATUE OF LIBERTY AND ELLIS ISLAND

Ferries for the Statue of Liberty and Ellis Island leave from **Battery Park**, calling first at the Statue of Liberty (www.statuecruises.com; daily 8.30am–5pm in summer, until 3.30pm in winter; departures every 20 mins).

The **Statue of Liberty** ❹ is the most recognized icon of New York City. Some 10 years in the making, it was a gift from France in recognition of the friendship between the two countries and has served as a beacon for immigrants arriving in the New World for over 100 years. Frédéric-Auguste Bartholdi's 151ft (46m) tall creation is one of those wild dreams that became reality. Engineering expertise had to be harnessed to art, so Bartholdi called in Gustave Eiffel to work on the complex skeletal framework. Parisian workmen erected the statue in 1884, as bemused Parisians watched her crowned head

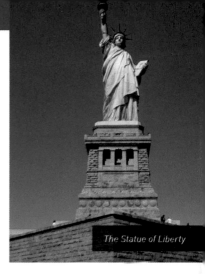
The Statue of Liberty

rise above their rooftops. It was later dismantled and shipped in 214 huge wooden crates for re-assembly on Liberty Island. The statue of Liberty Enlightening the World was unveiled by President Cleveland on October 28, 1886.

There are three options for visiting the monument and all must be booked through Statue Cruises (www.statuecruises. com). A basic cruise ticket will get you to Liberty Island, but you will need one of two additional tickets to enter the statue. Most choose a pedestal ticket, which grants access to the base and its museum. A few hundred daily crown tickets are available for those who plan ahead and are able to climb the steep steps to the top of the crown. Please note that many restrictions apply to crown tickets, including minimum height requirements.

Once you arrive on Liberty Island you can learn about the history of the statue with free tours led by Park Rangers. Inside the lobby visitors can view the original torch in The Torch Exhibit, then proceed to the promenade area for an up-close view of the statue and a spectacular view of New York Harbor. It is a strenuous climb up the 377 narrow steps to the crown but if you're lucky enough to snag a ticket, you'll be rewarded with a great view. The torch remains closed to the public as it has been since 1916.

After the statue, the ferry continues to **Ellis Island ⑤**. The island itself was mostly created from landfill from the building of the New York subway system. The museum, which opened in 1990, retraces, through film, audio-visual displays, and exhibitions, the sufferings and joys of some 12 million immigrants who entered the United States through these doors between 1892 and 1954, when overseas consulates took over the screening process. You might find a long lost family member on the Immigrant Wall of Honor. Among notable personalities who made it through Ellis

Fraunces Tavern

Island were actors Charlie Chaplin, Claudette Colbert, and Bob Hope, composer Irving Berlin, the Von Trapp family of *The Sound of Music* fame, and author Rudyard Kipling.

FRAUNCES TAVERN

Near the ferry terminal, at 54 Pearl Street (at Broad Street) is **Fraunces Tavern**. First opened for business in 1762, this is where George Washington is said to have bid farewell to his officers after the Revolutionary War. The building you see today is mostly a recreation, built in 1907. Colonial history buffs may appreciate the modest museum upstairs (www.frauncestavern-museum.org; Mon–Fri noon–5pm, Sat–Sun 11am–5pm): exhibits include documents and period furniture, as well as items such as a lock of Washington's hair, a fragment of one of his teeth, and a shoe that belonged to his wife, Martha. Others may opt to dine in the pseudo-colonial atmosphere of the restaurant downstairs, together with bankers and brokers (daily 11am–2am).

The immediate area is absolutely teeming with remnants of old New York. After leaving Fraunces Tavern, if you walk to the right on Pearl Street and turn left at the next corner, you'll come to **Stone Street**, another historic district with a colonial street plan and buildings that were formerly dry goods warehouses and stores. At the other end of Stone Street, after a quick jog to the right, you will be back on Pearl Street and Hanover Square, which was a wealthy neighborhood during colonial days. Two blocks south of the tavern, at the end of Broad Street, you will find the southern tip of the island and the terminal for the ferries to Staten Island and Governor's Island (www.govisland.com; daily May–Oct).

WALL STREET

If you continue on Pearl Street, after a couple of blocks you will come to **Wall Street ❻**, perhaps one of the most famous streets in the world, if only for its metaphoric heft. There was once an actual wall here, built in 1653 by Dutch governor Peter Stuyvesant to protect New Amsterdam from the encroaching British. Turn left on Wall Street to find several buildings of note. Number 55 Wall Street, which dates to 1842, is one of the oldest buildings on the street. The tallest, at 927ft (283m), is 40 Wall Street. Now known as the **Trump Building**, this was briefly the world's tallest structure, before it was eclipsed by the Chrysler

Building's spire. The skyscrapers here are closer together than at any other place in the city, leading locals to dub them the 'canyons' of Lower Manhattan.

At 26 Wall Street (at Nassau), you will see a large statue of Washington outside **Federal Hall National Memorial** (www.nps.gov/feha; Mon–Sat 9am–5pm), which was formerly the US Customs building. The original building, demolished in 1812, was the home of the US government for a year when New York was briefly the nation's capital (1785–90); it was also where Washington took the oath as the first president of the US, on April 30, 1789.

Most visitors to the city are more interested in the building across the street, the **New York Stock Exchange**, at 8–18 Broad Street. Interestingly, though Wall Street is synonymous with stock trading, the building's entrance is on the cross street. The NYSE is no longer open to the public for visits or tours.

BROOKLYN BRIDGE

There are a few other sights of interest to visitors in Lower Manhattan. At the corner of Broadway and Fulton streets is **St Paul's Chapel** and its churchyard. George Washington worshiped here after his inauguration; you can see the pew in which he sat, to your right as you enter.

A little farther up at 233 Broadway stands the **Woolworth Building**, which reigned as the world's tallest building from 1913 until the Chrysler Building ushered in the skyscraper age in 1930. You can't go upstairs, but take a look at the ornate lobby. Just up Broadway is **New York City Hall**, which is fairly unassuming. And if you are in the mood for a stroll, there is none more scenic or interesting than a trip by foot across the **Brooklyn Bridge** ❼, which opened in 1883. Before it was built, the only way across to Brooklyn was by ferry. The entrance to

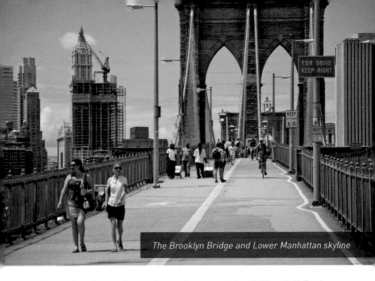

The Brooklyn Bridge and Lower Manhattan skyline

the pedestrian walkway is on the east side of City Hall Park; take a walk all the way to Brooklyn Heights.

One more detour may be in order for history buffs. At 241 Water Street is the **Seamen's Church Institute**, which has a gallery and ship models. However, many are drawn to the area for what lies across the street, the **Titanic Memorial Lighthouse**, erected in memory of those lost on the ill-fated ocean liner.

SOUTH STREET SEAPORT

A final area of interest in this part of Lower Manhattan is the **South Street Seaport**. At the foot of Fulton Street on the East River, this 11-acre (4-hectare), nine-block enclave was once in the middle of the nation's busiest working docks. Yet its usefulness faded, and the area was turned into a pedestrian mall in the 1960s. The **South Street Seaport Museum**, (www.southstreetseaportmuseum.org;

Wed–Sun 11am–7pm) at 12 Fulton Street, offers a glimpse into the nautical heritage of the city.

Occupying **Pier 17** ❽ is a glass fronted multi-use building overlooking the East River. Retail space houses top brands and restaurants as well as a Market Hall which offers healthy fast foods and produce. The roof top is open for concerts, cinema screenings and sports classes as well as hosting pop-up bars in the summer.

WEST MIDTOWN – THEATER DISTRICT

When visitors think of New York and the Big Apple, this intersection of Broadway and Seventh Avenue is usually considered the center of it all. It is also the heart of the Broadway theater district.

TIMES SQUARE AND BROADWAY

Once a seedy, unpleasant place, **Times Square** ❾ lies at the intersection of Broadway and Seventh Avenue, at the heart of Manhattan's theater district. This is roughly the area between 42nd and 53rd streets, between Sixth and Eighth avenues.

◎ BROADWAY

The name Broadway is synonymous with glitz, glamour, theaters, shows, musicals and entertainment. The Great White Way, referring to the stretch between 40th and 53rd streets, takes its pseudonym from when it was first lit with electric lighting. Its heyday was in the 1920s and '30s, when there were over 80 theaters on and around Broadway. The most famous section was 42nd Street, so famous in fact that theater owners with properties on 41st or 43rd Street, built passageways through entire blocks just to be able to boast a 'Forty-Second Street' address.

Times Square

Back in the *Taxi Driver* years of the 1970s, it had reached a distinct low point. For a time, the area may have been the 'crossroads of the world,' but perhaps only for the down and out.

All that changed in the mid-1990s in Mayor Rudolf Giuliani's clean-up of the area. Gone are most of the hustlers, prostitutes, pornographic theaters and bookstores; in their place are smart office buildings, hotels, stores, restaurants, and other attractions that appeal to New Yorkers and tourists. Even the traffic jams are gone. Broadway from 47th to 42nd streets is now entirely pedestrianized. One can debate whether this change has made the area blander, but it certainly has been revived. The 'square' is named for the *New York Times*, whose headquarters was once at 1 Times Square, where the ball still drops on New Year's Eve. The *Times* has since moved premises twice, most recently to a 52-story skyscraper on 40th Street, but the square's name will probably never change. Other features of the square include the cylindrical NASDAQ Building at 43rd and Broadway, its huge electronic display providing up-to-the-minute financial news. At the corner of 44th Street is the Viacom building, where MTV's Times Square Studio is located. On the east side of the Square (also at 44th Street), is the corner studio for *Good Morning America*.

NORTH OF TIMES SQUARE

Across Broadway (between Seventh Avenue and Broadway at 47th Street), you can't miss the glowing red steps in **Father Duffy Square**, the northern triangle of Times Square. Enjoy a break on the steps as you watch the hustle and bustle of the Times Square. Under the steps you will find the TKTS booth, which offers discounted tickets for same-day Broadway and off-Broadway plays and musicals.

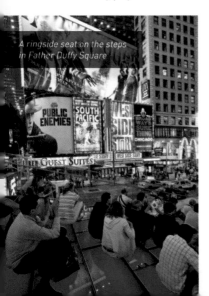

A ringside seat on the steps in Father Duffy Square

Further north at 1697 Broadway is the Ed Sullivan Theater, where *The Late Show with Stephen Colbert* is based. There is an official NYC Information Center for visitors at 810 Seventh Avenue (52nd and 53rd streets). At 131 W. 55th Street (between Sixth and Seventh avenues) is **City Center** (www.nycitycenter.org). Two blocks north is **Carnegie Hall** (154 W. 57th Street; www.carnegiehall.org), one of New York's most famous performing arts spaces;

the main concert hall (the Isaac Stern Auditorium) is said to have the best acoustics in New York.

WEST 42ND STREET

West of Times Square, on 42nd Street are some of the refurbished theaters and entertainment centers. On the north side of 42nd Street is the **New Victory Theater**, which specializes in children's productions; beyond the **Lyric Theatre** are two movie theaters facing each other across the street, the 13-screen **E Walk** entertainment complex and the 25-screen **AMC Empire**. On the south side of 42nd Street is a **Madame Tussaud's Wax Museum**. On the northeast corner of 42nd and Broadway is the **Condé Nast Building**, publisher of numerous glossy magazines.

Carnegie Hall

Financed by the iron and steel magnate Andrew Carnegie, Carnegie Hall was first opened in 1891. It is one of the great music venues of the city. If you can't make it to a concert here, at least have a look at the excellent museum.

At Eighth Avenue, is the **Port Authority of New York**, the city's main bus station. Once the scariest place in Manhattan, it is still not picturesque, but is a thriving and not unpleasant commuter hub. Today the neighborhood is dominated by the **New York Times Building**, completed in 2007; it ties with the Chrysler Building (see page 45) as the sixth-tallest building in New York.

At the far western end of 42nd Street, Pier 83 is the home to the **Circle Line**, which offers tours around Manhattan (see page 96). A little further north, on Pier 86, at 46th Street and Twelfth Avenue, is the popular **Intrepid Sea, Air & Space Museum** ❿ (www.intrepidmuseum.org; daily 10am–5pm, until 6pm on summer weekends). The Intrepid, a decommissioned US Navy aircraft carrier, is packed with exhibits on sea exploration and warfare, space travel, and aviation. You will also find here the submarine USS *Growler*, a Concorde supersonic airliner, and the space shuttle *Enterprise*.

CENTRAL MIDTOWN

Midtown has a wealth of cultural and shopping attractions, from art (MoMA), to literature (New York Public Library) and the department stores of Fifth Avenue.

BRYANT PARK

East of Times Square on 42nd Street, between Sixth and Fifth avenues, are the green and leafy expanses of **Bryant Park**, another great New York restoration project of the early 1990s. The present French-style layout of the park dates from the Great Depression, but by the 1980s it had become a no man's land of drug dealers night and day. Now it is one of midtown's most pleasant oases, where office workers gather in the summer months for lunch or just to relax. Next to the park is the **New York Public Library** ⑪ (www.nypl.org), a grand Beaux-Arts-style building that dates to 1911; two handsome, famous and much-photographed stone lions, Patience and Fortitude, flag its Fifth Avenue entrance.

Diamond District

West 47th is New York's Diamond District, an area dominated by mostly Orthodox Jewish diamond dealers; unbelievably, the majority of the diamonds that pass through New York find their way to this unassuming street. While this may be a good place to shop for diamonds, it is questionable as to whether or not you'll find any real bargains at the jewelry or 'discount' electronics stores.

One of the largest research library in the world, the structure houses several million books, almost as many manuscripts, and several vast reading rooms. The main reading room has been modernized, but nevertheless retains its original grandeur. Changing exhibitions are regularly mounted in the library's exhibition halls.

New York Public Library

ROCKEFELLER CENTER

The centerpiece of central Manhattan, covering 22 acres (9 hectares) between Fifth and Sixth avenues, from 47th to 51st streets, is **Rockefeller Center** ⑫. The buildings in this complex are linked by underground walkways and concourses, which are themselves filled with shops, a post office, and restaurants. Columbia University purchased the site in 1811 when it was still farmland. In 1928, John D. Rockefeller, a founder of the Standard Oil Company, asked the university for a lease on the site to raise a commercial complex. Built mostly between 1931 and 1940, Rockefeller Center attracts thousands of office-workers, visitors, and shoppers daily.

From Fifth Avenue you enter via the **Channel Gardens**, a sloping walkway divided by fountains and flowerbeds between the British and French buildings, which end at the sunken plaza and its famous ice rink and gilded **statue of Prometheus**. This is also where the giant Christmas tree is placed (right behind

Statue of Prometheus

Prometheus). If you have time, wander around and admire some of the Art Deco details.

Nowadays, the former GE Building, now **30 Rockefeller Center** or Comcast Building (30 Rockefeller Plaza, the largest building in the complex) is better known as the headquarters for the NBC television network and the *Today Show*; the glassed-in studio is across the street from the building's southeast corner, at 49th Street.

The Comcast's observation deck is called **Top of the Rock** (entrance on W. 50th Street; www.topoftherocknyc.com; daily 8am–12.30am), and offers visitors an unparalleled and unobstructed 360-degree view of the city from the 70th floor. The elevator to the top features a transparent ceiling so that visitors can view their rapid ascent all the way up the elevator chute. A light show and projected images add to the fun of the ride.

Also at this corner is the **NBC Experience**, a combination attraction and merchandise store festooned with the logos of the network and some of its television shows. You can also purchase tickets here for the extremely popular NBC Studio Tour (www.the touratnbcstudios.com; daily 8.20am–2.20pm, Fri until 5pm, with exceptions; tours every 20 mins).

Radio City Music Hall (corner of Sixth Avenue and 50th Street) is one of the largest theaters in the world, with a seating capacity of around 6,000. This restored Art Deco masterpiece is a popular location for seasonal theme shows, including the dazzling Christmas Spectacular; it's also the home of the ever-popular Rockettes. Tours can be arranged by tel: 866-858-0007, or at www.msg.com/radio-city-music-hall.

FIFTH AVENUE

At the turn of the 20th century, **Fifth Avenue** was the location of some of the largest and most opulent mansions in New York. After World War I, a number of fashionable and expensive stores opened for business here. You'll still find Saks Fifth Avenue (50th Street), Henri Bendel (55th and 56th streets), Tiffany's (57th Street), and Bergdorf Goodman (58th Street), though most of the trendiest designers now have their boutiques on Madison Avenue.

The gaudiest addition to Fifth Avenue has without a doubt been Donald Trump's **Trump Tower** (56th and 57th streets), where a 'wall' of water slides down rose marble set between gleaming brass escalator rails.

St Patrick's Cathedral ⓑ, on Fifth Avenue (50th and 51st), was the tallest building in the vicinity when it was built between 1858 and 1879. Today, it appears somewhat dwarfed by the skyscrapers of Rockefeller Center and the apartment building next door, though

The view from Top of the Rock

St Patrick's Cathedral

the juxtaposition of its soft gray granite and the surrounding glass creates a stunning image. Seat of the Archdiocese of New York City, the church is the focal point of the Irish parade on St Patrick's Day.

At the corner of Fifth Avenue and 59th Street, busy **Grand Army Plaza** marks the division between Fifth Avenue's shopping area and the residential section, which is lined with exclusive apartment buildings and a few remaining mansions. This is the place to hire a horse-drawn carriage for a ride round Central Park (see page 56). It is also the site of two of New York's most famous hotels, the **Plaza** and the **Pierre** (at East 61st Street).

Across from the plaza is the General Motors Building. A distinctive 32ft (10m) glass cube in front of it marks the entrance to the subterranean **Apple Store** (767 Fifth Avenue), where you can browse the latest cutting-edge iPads, iPhones, and other Apple products 365 days a year, 24 hours a day.

MUSEUM OF MODERN ART

One of midtown's most important cultural centers is the **Museum of Modern Art** ⑭, or MoMA (www.moma.org; daily 10.30am–5.30pm, Fri until 8pm, with exceptions), located on 53rd Street between Fifth and Sixth avenues. From 2002–2004, a complete redesign by architect Yoshio Taniguchi doubled the museum's exhibition space and now another major renovation is in the works, to be completed in 2019. The museum purchased the building next door – the former home of the American Folk Art Museum – in order to expand gallery space by 30 percent, thus being able to show more of their extensive collection and to increase public space, allowing for a more comfortable visitor experience. Shops, restaurants, cafes and coffee shops are being added and existing ones completely renovated. Public areas will include spaces to discuss art and visitors can see live performances in the art studio and performance center.

Devoted to works of art created after 1880, roughly from the Impressionists on, the collection includes such masterpieces as Dalí's *The Persistence of Memory*, Van Gogh's *The Starry Night*, Rousseau's *Sleeping Gypsy*, Wyeth's *Christina's World* and Warhol's *Gold Marilyn Monroe*. The collection also includes a number of Monet's Water Lilies, as well as important works by Picasso, Jackson Pollock, Mark Rothko and Chuck Close.

Modern sculpture and design is not ignored, and there are examples of everything from Marcel Duchamp's *Bicycle Wheel* to huge installations by contemporary artists. The modern sculpture garden remains a distinctive element of MoMA.

MoMA's sculpture gardens

Grand Central Terminal

The flagship MoMA design store, a great place to buy artistically designed household wares, is located within the museum; a second store is across the street at 44 West 53rd Street. There is a third in SoHo (81 Spring Street).

EAST MIDTOWN

In this area you will spend much of your time looking up at major architectural landmarks, including the ceiling of Grand Central and the Chrysler Building.

MADISON AND PARK AVENUES

The streets east of Fifth Avenue have several places of interest to visitors. The 57-story tower of the **Lotte New York Palace Hotel** (East 50th and 51st) incorporates the historic Villard Houses, which date to 1882. Take a walk through the grand lobby if you are in the area.

A Park Avenue landmark is the **Waldorf-Astoria Hotel**, which takes up the entire block between Park and Lexington from 49th to 50th. It has been host to world leaders since 1931. Nearby, the bronze-and-glass **Seagram Building**, on Park Avenue between 52nd and 53rd, is the only New York building designed by Mies van der Rohe. Across the street, at 390 Park Avenue, is the 24-story **Lever House**. Built in 1952 it was one of the first glass-walled office buildings in the States.

GRAND CENTRAL AND THE CHRYSLER BUILDING

A complete restoration and renovation project in the late 1990s returned **Grand Central Terminal** ⑮ (at 42nd between Park and Lexington) to its former splendor. Completed in 1913, the building is a Beaux-Arts masterpiece. Inside, more than 40 platforms split between two levels serve dozens of rail lines. The central concourse is vast but also light, airy, and harmonious under a blue-green, star-sprinkled ceiling 12 stories tall. It is invaded every afternoon from 4–6pm by hundreds of thousands of suburban commuters catching their trains home to points north of Manhattan. If you enter from the Vanderbilt Avenue side, look across the lobby to see the grand staircase. Inside the station are restaurants, shops, and, on the lower level, the famous **Oyster Bar & Restaurant**, a favorite for power-lunchers.

Across Lexington Avenue on 42nd Street stands the most beautiful skyscraper of all, the **Chrysler Building** ⑯, a silvery Art-Deco needle completed in 1930. For a few months it was the tallest structure in the world, but it

Touring Grand Central

75-minute tours of Grand Central Station are offered daily at 12.30pm by the Municipal Arts Society of New York (meet at the information booth on the Grand Concourse; tel: 212-935 3960; www.mas.org), and on Fridays free tours are conducted by the Grand Central Partnership (meet at 12.30pm in the sculpture court at 120 Park Avenue, located at the southwest corner of East 42nd Street and Park Avenue directly across from Grand Central Terminal; tel: 212-883 2420; www.grandcentralpartnership.nyc]. Alternatively, download an app for iPhone and Android phones at https://orpheogroup.com/us/the-official-grand-central-tour-app for a self-guided tour.

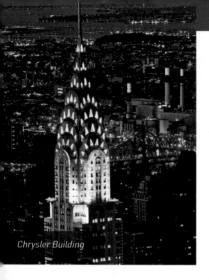

Chrysler Building

was rapidly surpassed by the Empire State Building (see page 47). The stylized eagle heads on the upper corners were modeled on the Chrysler automobile's 1929 radiator cap.

At the corner of Second Avenue, even more fine Art Deco architecture distinguishes the former **Daily News Building**; the lobby, with its huge revolving globe, is well worth a look. The paper moved to a new location west of Penn Station in the mid-1990s. Also well worth a look is the **Ford Foundation** headquarters (320 East 43rd Street); offices open onto a spacious interior court with trees – New York's first office building atrium. It's another of the city's fine public spaces.

UNITED NATIONS

The eastern end of 42nd Street used to be a warren of tenements and slaughterhouses, but thanks to John D. Rockefeller, Jr., it is now the home of the **United Nations** ⑰. A team of architects, including Wallace K. Harrison, Le Corbusier, and Oscar Niemeyer, designed the buildings. They were completed in the early 1950s. The Secretariat is housed in the glass-and-marble structure, while the General Assembly meets in the lower building with the slightly concave roof. The flags of the member nations flutter from the flagpoles along First Avenue.

When the General Assembly is not in session, visitors from around the world take daily multilingual tours (http://visit.un.org; guided tours year-round Mon–Fri 9am–4.45pm) of the General Assembly Hall and Council Chambers, the sculptures in the grounds overlooking the East River and Queens, and informative documentary exhibits. A highlight is the meditation room adorned with stained-glass windows by Chagall.

SOUTH MIDTOWN

EMPIRE STATE BUILDING

The **Empire State Building** ⓲ (corner of Fifth Avenue and 34th Street; www.esbnyc.com; daily 8am–2am) no longer holds the title of tallest building in the world. Yet, it is otherwise everything a skyscraper should be: 102 stories; 60,000 tons of steel; 3,500 miles (5,632km) of telephone wires and cables; 60 miles (97km) of pipes; a total volume of 1.25 million cubic yards (1 million cubic meters); 1,860 steps, and of course, its towering height – 1,453ft (443m), including the lightning rod (overall, half as tall again as the Eiffel Tower). It is a well-worn cultural icon, appearing in movies from *King*

The Empire State Building

Taking in the view from the Empire State's observation deck

Kong and *An Affair to Remember* to *Sleepless in Seattle*. Opened in 1931 in the depths of the Great Depression, the building took just two years to complete. The 86th-floor Observation Deck provides stunning views of New York. On the outside terrace you can see much of Manhattan, including Central Park, and on a clear day you can see ships 40 miles (64km) away. You can also visit the 102nd floor observatory (extra charge).

Back on earth, you can walk west along 34th Street to visit **Macy's** (Sixth and Seventh avenues), New York's most famous and largest department store. Nearby, at Seventh Avenue and 33rd Street, is **Madison Square Garden**, renowned for boxing matches and rock concerts. In addition to being home to the New York Knicks (basketball) and the Rangers (ice hockey), it is also used as a conference center. The Garden seats 20,000 people and its adjacent theater can take an additional 5,000. Under Madison Square Garden is Pennsylvania Station (usually referred to as Penn Station), the railway terminal for New Jersey and Long Island commuters and the Manhattan stop for Amtrak. Across Eighth Avenue is the **General Post Office**, which was a twin to the old Penn Station, torn down in the late 1960s to make room for Madison Square Garden. Moynihan Station, an expansion of Penn Station under Eighth Avenue, is underway with phase one, the West End Concourse, already complete and phase two set for completion in 2021, along with a new rail tunnel below the Hudson River which will be linked to Penn Station.

If you are in town for a trade show, chances are that you will head for the **Jacob K. Javits Convention Center** (www. javitscenter.com), the city's largest exhibition center, a striking building on Eleventh Avenue between 34th and 37th streets. Designed by I. M. Pei, the center was named for New York state's long-time Republican senator.

⊙ CITYPASS

One way to see several of Manhattan's top attractions and to save some money at the same time is to buy a CityPass. The pass gives you admission to six leading attractions for only $126, considerably less than the total for individual full admission prices. Attractions include the Empire State Building Observation Deck, the Metropolitan Museum of Art, the American Museum of Natural History, the Guggenheim Museum or Top of the Rock, Circle Line Sightseeing Cruises or Statue of Liberty and Ellis Island and 9/11 Memorial and Museum or the Intrepid Sea, Air & Space Museum. The pass can be used for nine consecutive days and should enable you to avoid most ticket lines. Buy it online at www.citypass.com, or at any of the participating attractions.

To the east of the Empire State Building, at 36th and Madison in Murray Hill, is another prominent landmark: the **Morgan Library & Museum** (www.themorgan.org). The personal collection of J. Pierpont Morgan includes rare books and manuscripts, three Gutenberg Bibles and Florentine sculpture and art. Often overlooked by tourists, it is a quiet place, which is one of its pleasures.

UPPER EAST SIDE – THE MUSEUM MILE

Home to many famous museums, the Upper East Side starts at 59th Street, at the corner of Central Park. Beyond the east 60s, much of this area is residential, and includes some of Manhattan's most expensive real estate.

Asia Society

The attractive redgranite building on the northeast corner of Park Avenue and 70th Street is the headquarters of the Asia Society (www.asiasociety.org; Tue–Sun 11am–6pm, Fri until 9pm, with exceptions). The society mounts regular, imaginative exhibitions of ancient and modern Asian and Pacific art, assembled from private collections, as well as from its own permanent collection.

Most of the Upper East Side's museums are located along the 'Museum Mile' from 82nd to 110th streets. But there are a few exceptions. One is the **Mount Vernon Hotel Museum and Garden**, at 421 East 61st Street (First and York avenues; www.mvhm.org; Tue–Sun 11am–4pm). This Federal-style house, which dates from 1799, is an interesting period piece for those with time and interest, featuring 19th-century furnishings and decorative arts.

FRICK COLLECTION

A few other major museums are just off the Museum Mile proper. The **Frick Collection** at 70th Street and Fifth Avenue (www.frick.org; Tue–Sat 10am–6pm, Sun 11am–5pm) is situated in the former mansion of coal and steel baron Henry Clay Frick, who put together one of the finest private collections of art in the US (mostly European paintings and sculpture). Upon the death of Frick's widow in 1931, their

The Garden Court at Frick mansion

home, which was designed by Thomas Hastings, and the art therein, were donated to the city of New York as a museum; it opened in 1935 after a reconstruction designed by John Russell Pope. Visitors have the pleasure of seeing not only beautiful works of art but also the mansion and its gardens, much as they were when the Fricks lived there; it is a rare and wonderful experience. In addition to three Vermeers (including *Mistress and Maid*), the museum holds fine works by Hans Holbein (*Sir Thomas More* and *Thomas Cromwell*), El Greco (*St. Jerome*), Bellini (*St. Francis in Ecstasy*), Boucher, Titian, Goya, Whistler, Rembrandt, and Velázquez; exquisite European furniture; and one of the largest collections of small bronze sculptures in the world.

METROPOLITAN MUSEUM OF ART

Museum Mile begins at the **Metropolitan Museum of Art** ②, located at 82nd Street and Fifth Avenue (www.metmuseum.org;

Sun–Thu 10am–5.30pm, Fri–Sat 10am–9pm). Monumentally huge, the 'Met,' as it is affectionately known, is a repository for all things cultural, from Egyptian mummies to Roman bronzes, Chinese pottery and wonderful Impressionist paintings. Founded in 1870, the institution owns over 2 million items, though only around a quarter of the total collection is on display at any one time in its nearly 250 rooms. The Art of the Arab Lands galleries are worth a closer look, especially the textiles and the stunning 16th-century decorative ceiling of interlocking stars and polygons. More than 5,300 works of classical art are on show in the refurbished Greek and Roman galleries. Children love the Egyptian treasures, especially the Temple of Dendur, which sits in its own room.

Don't miss the American Wing, particularly the Garden Court, where stained-glass windows, fountains, sculptures, plants and

The Metropolitan Museum of Art

benches create a tran-
quil environment. On all
sides are period rooms
and other galleries that
show off the Met's fine
holdings in American art.
Among the famous paint-
ings are Emanuel Leutze's
*Washington Crossing the
Delaware*, Albert Bierstadt's
The Rocky Mountains, as
well as notable works by
Winslow Homer.

*Portrait of Adele Bloch-
Bauer I by Gustav Klimt in
the Neue Galerie*

European paintings,
sculpture, and decorative
arts before 1000 include
Botticelli's *Last Communion of St. Jerome*, Giovanni di Paolo's
Adoration of the Magi, Rembrandt's *Self-Portrait*, 1660, and
works by Bellini, Ingres, El Greco, Holbein, Goya, and virtually
any other famous painter you can name. Similarly stellar is the
collection of 19th-century European paintings and sculptures,
including works by such luminaries as Van Gogh, Monet, Renoir,
and Degas. The Robert Lehman Collection, at the west end of the
main floor, comprises fine Old Masters and Italian Renaissance
paintings, including several period rooms recreated from
Lehman's home. The Michael C. Rockefeller Wing houses a good
collection of primitive art.

The Lila Acheson Wallace Wing, devoted to modern art, remains
one of the most popular sections of the Met. It features paintings, sculptures, and decorative arts from Europe and America,
including Picasso's *Gertrude Stein* and works by major modern
artists including Jackson Pollock, Willem de Kooning, Edward

Special exhibitions

Visitors should look out for special exhibitions at the Met; your standard entry will cover admission and no additional ticket is required to see them.

Hopper, Georgia O'Keefe, Diego Rivera, Frank Stella, and Chuck Close. Modern sculpture is often on view in the roof garden overlooking Central Park, where there is a café in the summer. On top of all this, the Met has one of the best art bookstores in the US.

NEUE GALERIE

Four blocks north of the Met (1048 Fifth Avenue at 86th Street) is the **Neue Galerie** (www.neuegalerie.com; Thu–Mon 11am–6pm), a small but unique museum that specializes in early 20th-century German and Austrian art and design, featuring works by Gustav Klimt and various Bauhaus exponents. It is housed in an elegant mansion built in 1914 for the industrialist William Starr Miller by Carrère and Hastings, architects of the New York Public Library; the building was once occupied by society doyenne, Mrs Cornelius Vanderbilt III. The Café Sabarsky inside (see page 113) is a recommended stop too.

More 20th and 21st century art can be seen at The Met Breuer (Tue–Sun 10am–5.30pm, Fri–Sat until 9pm) located on Madison Avenue and 75th Street in a landmark building designed by Marcel Breuer.

GUGGENHEIM MUSEUM

At 89th Street is the **Solomon R. Guggenheim Museum** ㉑ (www.guggenheim.org; Sun–Wed and Fri 10am–5.45pm, Sat 10am–7.45pm, with exceptions). The building, which was designed by Frank Lloyd Wright and opened in 1959, is now a New York landmark. The museum's most famous feature is perhaps not its paintings but the continuous spiral ramp that connects the building's six storeys.

The permanent collection, built on Guggenheim's original private collection of contemporary paintings, includes works by such artists as Brancusi, Klee, Chagall, Picasso, Miró, Calder, and Kandinsky. The Justin K. Thannhauser collection, in the annex, contains paintings by Renoir, Monet, Cézanne, Van Gogh, Gauguin, and Degas. The museum's collection is actually now spread somewhat thinly among its various branches in such disparate places as Bilbao, Las Vegas, Venice, and Berlin.

OTHER MUSEUMS

Nearby, at 91st Street, is the **Cooper-Hewitt, Smithsonian Design Museum** (www.cooperhewitt.org; daily 10am–6pm, Sat until 9pm). A branch of the Smithsonian Institution, the Cooper-Hewitt is more of a research institution than a museum, with vast holdings of furniture, wall-coverings, textiles, prints, drawings, and miscellaneous objects.

The Guggenheim

At 92nd Street, the **Jewish Museum** (www.jewishmuseum.org; Fri–Tue 11am–5.45pm, Thu until 8pm, free Sat), housed in a gothic mansion, is an important cultural and historical museum. It holds an extensive collection of Judaica and exhibits the work of Jewish artists.

The **Museum of the City of New York** (www.mcny.org; daily 10am–6pm) is located at 103rd Street. This treasury of materials documenting New York City's history also includes a superb toy collection. The last institution on Museum Mile is **El Museo del Barrio** (www.elmuseo.org; Tue–Sat 11am–6pm, Sun noon–5pm), at 104th Street. Americans of Hispanic origin live in many parts of the city's boroughs, but El Barrio – the Quarter – in East (or Spanish) Harlem was the first predominantly Puerto Rican district. The museum is devoted to Latin American culture and art.

The long-gestating **Africa Center** (www.theafricacenter.org), a successor of the former Museum for African Art, at 110th Street has extended the Museum Mile to the northeastern tip of Central Park. Check their website for opening details.

CENTRAL PARK

The heart (some say the lungs) of Manhattan is **Central Park**, located between 59th and 110th streets and Fifth and Eighth avenues. This vast green space is half a mile wide and 2.5 miles long (0.8km x 4km) and is one of the main places where New Yorkers go to play. On summer weekends, residents (and visitors) come by the thousands to play ball, skate, stroll, picnic, or listen to music. But the park is busy all week and all year long. The park's designers were Frederick Law Olmsted and Calvert Vaux, and the project, which began in 1858, took almost 20 years to complete. Creating a usable public space from a huge, sparse, and rocky landscape was a remarkable achievement for the time and revolutionized landscape architecture. Amazingly, almost everything you see in the park today, from the Great Lawn to the lakes, to the meadows and forest in the northern end, was constructed. The

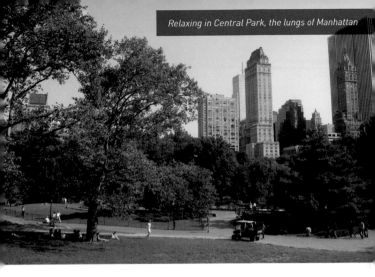
Relaxing in Central Park, the lungs of Manhattan

park is now partially supported, administered, and overseen by the Central Park Conservancy (www.centralparknyc.org).

There is always something going on in the park, from a concert to a rally to a bicycle race. To learn more about the park you can take a walking tour. The Central Park Conservancy sponsors free guided tours year-round, rain or shine, and downloadable audio tours (see the schedule and find downloads at www.centralparknyc.org). The more active will be interested in ball fields, tennis courts, and other sporting opportunities. Since most of the park's roads are closed on weekends, strolling, biking, and skating are popular.

PARK HIGHLIGHTS

Highlights in the southern end of the park include **Wollman Rink** (mid-Park at 63rd Street), which is used for ice-skating in the winter. A children's amusement park takes over during the summer months. There's another skating rink in the northern end of the park, Lasker Rink (between W. 106th and 108th streets), which is transformed into a very popular swimming pool in the summer.

Closer to Fifth Avenue is the **Central Park Zoo ㉒**, including the **Tisch Children's Zoo** (www.centralparkzoo.com; Apr–Oct Mon–Fri 10am–5pm, Sat–Sun 10am–5.30pm, Nov–Mar daily 10am–4.30pm). In between is the Delacorte Musical Clock, which chimes the hours with musical animals. The highlights of the zoo include the sea-lion pool and polar bear house. Kids will love the petting zoo and the 'Enchanted Forest.' The admission charge for Central Park Zoo includes entrance to the children's zoo, and both are open daily.

Another favorite in the southeast corner of the park is the historic **Carousel**, located mid-Park at 64th Street. It dates from 1908 and used to stand in a Coney Island amusement park. You can still ride it, weather permitting (Apr–Oct daily 10am–6pm, Nov–Mar call for hours 718-373 5862).

On the park's west side, near 66th Street, is **Tavern on the Green**. The gardens and building are dazzling and house an information center and a restaurant serving local and artisanal food. Nearby is the **Sheep Meadow**, a popular spot for playing Frisbee and for sunbathing in summer; it is also a great place for a picnic. The sheep that used to graze here were originally

The Dairy

You might want to drop in at the Dairy (mid-Park at 65th Street; daily 9am–7.30pm), the Central Park visitors' center. The attractive Victorian Gothic structure was actually built as a dairy in 1870 in order to provide fresh milk to families. Today it displays a permanent exhibit on the park's history and design and provides visitors with brochures and information.

housed in the Tavern on the Green building.

Right in the middle of the park, beginning at 66th Street, is the **Literary Walk**, lined with statues of writers you will, for the most part, recognize. The path leads up to the Mall, where there is a band shell, and ends at the **Bethesda Terrace and Fountain**, one of the park's best-known spots. On the lake is the Loeb Boathouse, where there is

Central Park's ice rink

a café in addition to a good, though fairly expensive, restaurant. You can rent a boat or a bike near here in the summer.

To the east is the **Conservatory Water**, a pond where hobbyists sail model boats. At its northern end (at 74th Street) sits Central Park's most beloved sculpture, a bronze grouping of characters from Lewis Carroll's *Alice's Adventures in Wonderland*.

To the west is **Strawberry Fields**, a poignant memorial to John Lennon, who on December 8, 1980 was shot and killed outside the nearby Dakota apartment building at 72nd Street and Central Park West.

North (at 80th Street) is the **Delacorte Theatre**, best known as the stage for the summer's free Shakespeare in the Park productions.

In the center of the park is **Belvedere Castle** ㉓, which affords excellent views; inside is a nature center and weather station. From the Castle, you will be able to see the central

Walkers in the park

part of the park, which features the **Great Lawn**, popular with sun worshippers. On the east side is the Metropolitan Museum of Art (see page 51), and just to the south is **Cleopatra's Needle** (at 81st Street), a 3,600-year-old obelisk that was a gift from Egypt in the 19th century.

North of here are several other notable features. The gravel path around the **Jacqueline Kennedy Onassis Reservoir** (mid-Park, north of 86th Street) is a favorite with joggers. The **North Meadow** (mid-Park, at 96th Street) is another open expanse, and often serves as the site of free concerts. At 104th Street is the **Conservatory Garden**. At the northern end of the park on the east side is the **Harlem Meer**, a lake.

UPPER WEST SIDE

Beginning at **Columbus Circle**, where Broadway and Eighth Avenue (thereafter renamed Central Park West) converge, the Upper West Side stretches north to Columbia University (about 110th Street); its western boundary is the Hudson River and Riverside Park; its eastern boundary is Central Park. Columbus Circle is invigorated by the towering Time Warner Center that overlooks Central Park; the center includes the headquarters of Time Warner (including CNN), a retail complex, the Mandarin

Oriental Hotel, a collection of restaurants – including some of the biggest names in fine dining (including Thomas Keller's Per Se) – and the home of Jazz at Lincoln Center.

At 2 Columbus Circle is the **Museum of Arts and Design** (www.madmuseum.org; Tue–Sun 10am–6pm, Thu until 9pm) and its collection of everything from teapots to antique quilts and rocking chairs.

LINCOLN CENTER

The cultural epicenter of the Upper West Side is the **Lincoln Center for the Performing Arts** ㉔ (www.lincolncenter.org), which is bounded by 62nd and 66th streets (on the south and north), Amsterdam (the continuation of Tenth Avenue) on the west, and Columbus (the continuation of Ninth Avenue) on the east. The Center covers an area of 16 acres (7 hectares). The central plaza, a vast esplanade surrounding a fountain, acts as the focal point for the three main buildings. Built in 1960, the whole space is in the midst of a vast modernization program.

In the center is the **Metropolitan Opera House** (the other 'Met'), home to the Metropolitan Opera. The opera house was designed by Wallace K. Harrison and completed in 1966. It can hold nearly 4,000 people. Two Chagall murals

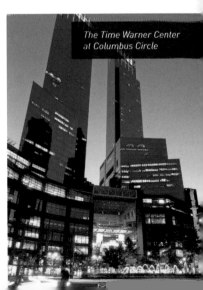

The Time Warner Center at Columbus Circle

Lincoln Center for the Performing Arts

adorning the central lobby can be seen from the outside. To the left of the Met is the **David H. Koch Theater**, home of the New York City Ballet and sometimes the American Ballet Theater. Designed by architect Philip Johnson and built in 1964, it has a simple, stately facade complemented by a red-and-gold auditorium studded with crystal; the notoriously bad acoustics were upgraded through the installation of a modern sound system. To the right of the Met, opposite the David H. Koch Theater, is **David Geffen Hall**, completed in 1962, which is primarily used for music concerts.

Just behind David Geffen Hall, you can make out the outline of **Vivian Beaumont Theater**, the only uptown stage for Broadway plays. Across 65th Street is the **Walter Reade Theater**, where the Film Society of Lincoln Center screens movies.

The **American Folk Art Museum** (2 Lincoln Square; www.folkartmuseum.org; Tue–Thu and Sat 11.30am–7pm, Fri noon–7.30pm, Sun noon–6pm) celebrates the 'extraordinary accomplishments of ordinary people.' The museum has exhibits ranging from 18th- and 19th-century paintings, to quilts and contemporary sculpture.

Farther back, but connected to Lincoln Center by a footbridge over West 65th Street, is the Juilliard School, one of the world's outstanding music conservatories.

Farther north are several interesting things to see. The Ansonia, at 2109 Broadway (73rd and 74th streets), is a notable Beaux-Arts apartment building. A little farther west, at the corner of 72nd and Central Park West, is the **Dakota**, which dates to 1884; it has been home to such rich and famous residents as John Lennon and Lauren Bacall and was the setting for the 1968 film *Rosemary's Baby*.

A few blocks farther north, between 76th and 77th streets, is the **New York Historical Society** (www.nyhistory.org; Tue–Sat 10am–6pm, Fri until 8pm, Sun 11am–5pm), the oldest museum in New York (the second-oldest in the US). In addition to documents and artifacts of historical interest, the Society's collection includes a collection of American fine and decorative arts.

NATURAL HISTORY MUSEUM

The huge building on Central Park West at 79th Street is the **American Museum of Natural History** ㉕ (www.amnh.org; daily 10am–5.45pm), another of New York's oldest museums, dating to 1869. Once considered a pretty stuffy place full of old dinosaur bones and dusty taxidermy displays, much of the museum has been reinvented over the past couple of decades and it is now one of the city's most popular collections; crowds are drawn to the **Hayden Planetarium**, the centerpiece of the Frederick Phineas and Sandra Priest Rose Center for Earth and Space. Its Journey to the Stars is an exciting and informative theatrical experience that introduces all ages to the creation of the universe and our solar system.

With tens of millions of specimens and artifacts, the museum is a repository for knowledge about virtually any aspect of earth's natural history and development. The creaking dioramas are still there and now seem quaint, but the refurbished parts of the museum have the most up-to-the-minute scientific information and wonderful state-of-the-art exhibitions. Examples of this are the Fossil Halls – covering everything from dinosaurs to mammals – and the Hall of Biodiversity, which includes a life-size recreation of a rainforest.

Don't miss the full-size model of a blue whale, the Star of India (the largest sapphire that has ever been discovered), and the Barosaurus in the Theodore Roosevelt Rotunda on Central Park West: standing on its rear legs, this long-necked sauropod is the tallest free-standing dinosaur exhibit in the world.

Tours of the collection's highlights are given regularly throughout the day and there are always a few special exhibitions worth visiting. The museum also has a massive IMAX theater.

COLUMBIA UNIVERSITY AREA

Many visitors are surprised to find one of the largest neo-Gothic cathedrals in the world in New York City. The **Episcopal Cathedral Church of St John the Divine**, at Amsterdam Avenue and 112th Street (www.stjohndivine.org; daily 7.30am–6pm, sightseeing tours Mon–Sat 9am–5pm, Sun 1–3pm), was begun in 1892 and is yet to be completed. The church is well known for its jazz and choral music series, in addition to its rotating art exhibits.

Beyond the cathedral, at 116th and Broadway, lies the campus of **Columbia University**. Founded in 1754 as King's College, Columbia is New York City's representative in the Ivy League. A private university, its schools of law and journalism and the

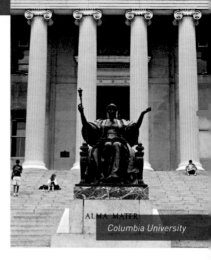

THE LIBRARY OF COLUMBIA UNIVERSITY

ALMA MATER

Columbia University

teacher's college are widely recognized for their excellence. The School of Journalism is perhaps most famous for administering the Pulitzer Prizes. The campus itself is striking. Right across Broadway stands Barnard College, Columbia University's affiliated women's college.

Close by, in Riverside Park at West 122nd Street, is **Grant's Tomb** ㉖, the mausoleum of Ulysses S. Grant. Here lies the commanding General of the Union Army in the Civil War and US President (1869–1877), alongside his wife, Julia Dent Grant. After the war, the general settled in New York City, worked on Wall Street and died here in July 1885. Administered by the National Park Service, the mausoleum, which is the biggest in the US, contains a museum devoted to Grant's life (visits Wed–Sun 10–11am, noon–1pm, 2–3pm, 4–5pm; visitors' center open Wed–Sun 9am–5pm).

HARLEM AND NORTH MANHATTAN

A major African-American cultural, spiritual and business center, **Harlem** continues to undergo an economic renaissance and rapid gentrification. It is a vital and varied community with rich, poor and middle-income sections, historical landmarks and attractive homes.

A popular way to see Harlem is on one of the hop-on-hop-off double-decker bus tours, or on a specialized tour that often includes lunch and a gospel music performance. Tours that include a Sunday church service are especially popular. For more information, see page 123.

Harlem begins north of Central Park at 110th Street and extends to 178th Street, bounded on the west by Morningside Heights and Washington Heights and on the north and east by the Harlem River, which connects the Hudson and East rivers. The neighborhood's commercial center is 125th Street, where you'll find the historic **Apollo Theater** (253 West 125th Street; www.apollotheater.org).

AN HISTORIC DISTRICT

Founded by Dutch settlers, Harlem remained a village for a long time. As immigrants moved into the Lower East Side, many middle-class families moved north to Harlem. The influx of black families started around 1900 and reached its height around 1920, when the area became a cultural hub and home to prominent artists and writers associated with the Harlem Renaissance. Historic row houses of this period are preserved

⊙ HARLEM'S CHURCHES

Central Harlem is known for its beautiful churches. The Abyssinian Baptist Church at 132 Odell Clark Place (aka West 138th Street) was founded in 1808; its current Harlem home dates to 1923. Also in the area is the Mother AME Zion Church, at 146 West 137th Street, which is the oldest African-American church in New York. St Philip's Episcopal Church is a striking neo-Gothic building at 204 West 134th Street.

Historic Harlem

in the **St Nicholas Historic District** between Adam Clayton Powell, Jr. Boulevard and Frederick Douglass Boulevard on 138th and 139th streets.

There are several prominent cultural institutions in the area. The **Studio Museum in Harlem** ㉗ (144 West 125th Street, at Lenox Avenue; www.studiomuseum.org; closed for renovation, see website for temporary location), is dedicated to African-American, Caribbean, and contemporary and traditional African art. At Malcolm X Boulevard and 135th Street, the **Schomburg Center for Research in Black Culture** (Mon–Sat 10am–6pm, Tue–Wed until 8pm), a branch of the New York Public Library and an art museum, has one of the world's most important collections covering black history and African-American culture.

North of Harlem is the **Hamilton Grange National Memorial**, which was the early 19th-century home of Founding Father Alexander Hamilton. The house was renovated and moved to St

Nicholas Park in 2011. The surrounding area, roughly between St Nicholas and Edgecombe avenues and 143rd to 155th streets, was once Hamilton's farm. It is now known as **Hamilton Heights** and is home to a historic area that includes the Sugar Hill row houses. The **Morris-Jumel Mansion** and gardens (1765) at 65 Jumel Terrace (near 162nd street) exhibits period furniture (www.morrisjumel.org; Tue–Sun 10am–4pm, Sat–Sun until 5pm).

The 1908 Beaux-Arts style **Audubon Terrace** complex, on Broadway between 155th and 156th streets, is home to two cultural institutions. The **American Academy of Arts and Letters** (www.artsandletters.org) has seasonal exhibitions, but is otherwise not open to the public. The **Hispanic Society of America** has a permanent collection that includes rare books and manuscripts and works by Goya and El Greco. Entrance to the society's library and museum is free to the public (www.hispanicsociety.org; closed for renovation).

Eating in Harlem

If you yearn for something to eat in Harlem, there are many good choices. The place that says Harlem for most people is Sylvia's (328 Lenox Avenue, at 127th Street, tel: 212-996 0660; www.sylviasrestaurant.com), where you can sample typical South Carolina fare; its Sunday gospel brunch is especially popular. Another popular eatery is Amy Ruth's (113 West 116th Street, tel: 212-280 8779; www.amyruths.com).

WASHINGTON HEIGHTS

Above Harlem, Manhattan narrows to a little sliver made up of **Washington Heights** and Inwood. Both are primarily residential neighborhoods, but there are a couple of interesting attractions. Washington Heights was long known as a drug-seller's haven, but it has cleaned up its act and is welcoming a diverse set of new residents who are joining the large Dominican population.

THE CLOISTERS

Beyond Washington Heights is **Fort Tryon Park**, 66 acres (26 hectares) of landscaped and terraced hills, which begins at 190th Street. From the subway stop (A line), it's possible to walk through the park to **The Cloisters** ㉘ (www.metmuseum.org; daily Mar–Oct 10am–5.15pm,

The Cloisters

Nov–Feb 10am–4.45pm). Part of the Metropolitan Museum (your admission to the Met also gives you same-day admission here), this branch is devoted to Medieval art and architecture. It is built around parts of several actual cloisters and other medieval structures. The views of the Hudson River from the outdoor terraces are breathtaking, and the gardens provide a great place to sit in reflective solitude.

Housed within The Cloisters are several genuine master-pieces, including the wood sculpture *Enthroned Virgin and Child*, a set of 'nine heroes' tapestries, a 12th-century carved ivory cross, and the museum's most popular holding, a set of tapestries depicting the *Hunt of the Unicorn*.

Not far away is the **Dyckman Farmhouse Museum** at 4881 Broadway (www.dyckmanfarmhouse.org; Thu–Sat 11am–4pm; until 3pm on Sun), the only remaining Dutch colonial farm-house in Manhattan. If you are in the area, it's worth a detour.

OTHER NEIGHBORHOODS

THE LOWER EAST SIDE

At the turn of the 20th century, the Lower East Side of Manhattan was the most densely populated place in the US, home to around half a million Russian and Eastern European Jewish immigrants. The remnants of the old Jewish neighborhood are located on the northeast side of Chinatown, beyond Hester Street, the site of the Jewish market at the end of the 19th century. Follow Hester Street east and then walk north along **Orchard Street**, and you'll see a shadow of the market's heyday mixed in with hip eateries and new clubs.

In this New World ghetto, the cornerstone of the economy was the 'needle trade.' Working conditions and pay were appalling. Those who didn't toil in the garment factories often worked as peddlers or pushcart vendors, selling produce or cheap clothing in the markets on Hester Street and Orchard Street. The **Lower East Side Tenement Museum** ㉙ at 97 Orchard Street offers an introduction to this area. The 19th-century tenement can be seen by guided tour only, and visitors view restored apartments of immigrant families in the tenement at different historical periods. Tours start from the Visitor Center, across the road at 103 Orchard Street (www.tenement.org; Fri–Wed 10am–6.30pm, Thu until 8.30pm, tour times vary; advance ticket purchase strongly recommended).

THE BOWERY

The Bowery is located on the eastern border of the Lower East Side. Once notorious as New York City's skid row, the Bowery and surrounding neighborhoods are filling up with luxury condominium buildings at a rapid pace. The Whole Foods Market (www.

wholefoodsmarket.com) at the corner of Bowery and Houston is always busy and a good place to take a break and grab a snack from a large selection of prepared foods. On the Bowery across from Prince Street is the **New Museum**, opened in 2007 (www. newmuseum.org; Tue–Sun 11am–6pm, Thu until 9pm) and the only one in the city devoted exclusively to contemporary art.

CHINATOWN

Of all the ethnic neighborhoods that were established on New York's Lower East Side, it is the Chinese enclave that has continued to thrive. The narrow shops sell ivory and jade jewelry, as well as bootleg designer watches and the usual souvenirs; grocers display exotic Chinese produce; and the area's innumerable restaurants feature a huge range of regional specialties. The earliest Chinese arrivals came here in the 19th century, after the California Gold Rush and the boom of railway construction. These days, the majority of Chinese immigrants actually live in Queens and Brooklyn, but many still work and play in bustling **Chinatown**, a loosely defined area embracing Canal Street, Chatham Square, and Mott Street. At 215 Centre Street is the **Museum of Chinese in America** ㉚ (www.mocanyc. org; Tue–Sun 11am–6pm, Thu until 9pm). In addition

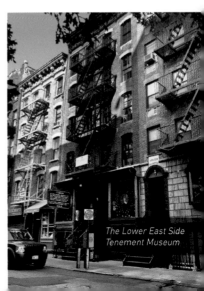

The Lower East Side Tenement Museum

to cultural programs and exhibitions, the museum conducts walking tours of the neighborhood.

Near Chatham Square, at the corner of Division Street and Bowery, stands a 1983 bronze statue of Confucius. South of the square, a few steps down St. James Place, are some of New York's oldest monuments, barely a dozen tombstones, the remnants of the **Shearith Israel Cemetery**, founded here in 1656 by New York's first immigrants, Spanish and Portuguese Jews.

LITTLE ITALY

'Little' is certainly the operative word here, as this area has now been largely subsumed by Chinatown. The stretch of Mulberry Street from Canal to Grand is still home to several Italian restaurants and expensive coffee bars. In the summer, especially on weekends, it is a pleasant place to stroll, buy a souvenir, and have a plate of pasta and a glass of house wine al fresco. There are still some good 'old world' bakeries and grocers here, though some of them, too, are now Chinese.

Chinatown dried goods

The district is at its liveliest during the ten-day Feast of San Gennaro in early September (see page 98). But if you find yourself in the neighborhood, you might want to take a stroll over to the old **Police Headquarters** at the corner of Centre and Grand streets; this is the building in which Theodore Roosevelt served as New York City's police commissioner. The inhabitants are now the tenants of the luxury condominiums created in the late 1980s.

SOHO AND TRIBECA

SoHo (South of Houston) is the area bound by Houston Street, Broadway, Canal Street, and the Hudson River. It has become the Village's chic southern neighbor, with expensive cafes, restaurants, art galleries, and shops selling the very latest in fashion and housewares.

The colors of Little Italy

Its history has followed the pattern of Greenwich Village. Artists who couldn't afford the rents after the Village's commercialization moved south to the derelict lofts and warehouse floors of the then industrial district. The most successful were able to install kitchens, bathrooms, and comfortable interiors, while others made do with bare walls and floors for the sake of ample space and light. Now the same lofts sell in the multi-million dollar range.

The main things to do here are to browse in the handful of remaining galleries, stop and relax at the many outdoor cafés and restaurants, and shop. There are plenty of interesting smaller boutiques located on side streets off Broadway, which is home to many big name designers and chain stores.

West Broadway is the quintessential SoHo street. Here you'll find the choicest boutiques and galleries. After SoHo became too expensive, the artists moved out, many heading southwest to the derelict warehouses of the **Tribeca** (Triangle Below Canal) neighborhood, which in its turn has inevitably seen the opening of upscale restaurants and trendy boutiques. As those rents began to soar, many of the artists migrated to Brooklyn and Queens and the art dealers moved to Chelsea.

GREENWICH VILLAGE

'The Village,' as **Greenwich Village** is usually called, has been separate, casual, and very different from the rest of the city ever since its beginnings. In colonial times it really was a distinct village called Greenwich, which became a neighborhood of conservative Georgian brick houses and carriage barns in back-alley mews. A few of these houses remain, mostly on **Bedford**

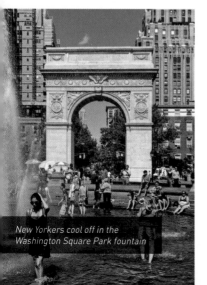

New Yorkers cool off in the Washington Square Park fountain

Street and the streets around it, but conservative the Village isn't. It got its bohemian reputation after World War I, when artists and writers moved here for the area's cheap lodgings, inexpensive restaurants and speakeasies. Later, the Village became the center for New York's gay community, which to a large degree has now moved north to Chelsea.

The Village is roughly the area from 14th Street down to Houston and west of Broadway. The area's heart is **Washington Square Park ㉛**, the de facto campus quad for **New York University**, which controls much of the real estate east of Sixth Avenue and south of 14th Street to Houston. The park's famous arch was designed by architect Stanford White and erected in 1889 to mark the centenary of George Washington's inauguration as president.

> ### De Niro's Tribeca
>
> Tribeca's expensive loft-style real estate is home to many high-profile New Yorkers. Perhaps the district's most ardent res-ident-supporter is actor Robert De Niro. He opened his restaurant Tribeca Grill, which is still going strong, and instituted the Tribeca Film Festival.

Bleecker Street with its craft and curio shops, antique stores, cafés, and tiny restaurants has long been the main shopping strip of the neighborhood. The area's highest concentration of gay and lesbian businesses and bars is still found on **Christopher Street**, west of Seventh Avenue South. The Stonewall, at 53 Christopher Street (now an official city's landmark), stands on the site of the original Stonewall Inn, which was the site of the riots in 1969 that led to the modern gay rights movement. You may wish to make at least two trips to the Village; by day to shop and see the sights, and at night to catch the atmosphere, have dinner, and hit one of the jazz clubs or bars.

EAST VILLAGE

A separate community, the **East Village** extends east from Broadway to Avenue D and the East River. Less affluent than Greenwich Village to the west, this neighborhood has never-theless fallen victim to plenty of gentrification and is probably the hippest place in Manhattan. You will find eclectic, edgy

The Gay Liberation statue
in Christopher Park

boutiques, restaurants, and shops that can't afford the other downtown rents. If there is any real bohemian spirit left in Manhattan, it may be here. Walk down St Mark's Place or Avenue A, the liveliest streets, or people-watch in Tompkins Square.

On Lafayette Street, just to the south of Cooper Square, stands the building that once housed the first public library of New York. Nowadays it is the seat of **The Public Theater**, which actually contains several theaters and is the host of Shakespeare in the Park. Joe's Pub, off the main lobby, is a celebrated venue for live music and performance. Nearby is the Great Hall of the Cooper Union, the center of the free university established by Peter Cooper in 1859.

Those interested in historic buildings might stop by **St Mark's-in-the-Bowery**, built in 1799 on the very spot where the Stuyvesant family chapel once stood (at 10th Street at Second Avenue). It is now a charming church with some noteworthy stained-glass windows and a spirited congregation, often hosting music or dance performances.

MEATPACKING DISTRICT AND CHELSEA

The northwest corner of Greenwich Village from West 14th Street to Gansevoort Street is a designated historic district of cobbled streets and warehouses. Home to a meat market during the last century, the area is now awash with trendy boutiques, restaurants, bars, clubs and hotels.

The **High Line** ❸❷ (www.thehighline.org; daily June–Sept 7am–11pm, Apr–May and Oct–Nov until 10pm, Dec–Mar until 7pm) is a major public park built on elevated railroad tracks. These tracks were originally constructed in the 1930s to lift freight trains off the streets of Manhattan. They have been converted into a beautifully landscaped walkway that stretches 1.45 miles (2.3km) from Gansevoort Street to West 34th Street and 10th Avenue, with multiple entrances and exits.

Housed in a striking building by architect Renzo Piano, the excellent **Whitney Museum of American Art** ❸❸ (http://whitney.org; Sun–Thu 10.30am–6pm, Fri–Sat until 10pm) was originally founded by Gertrude Vanderbilt Whitney, an artist from one of

⊙ VILLAGE VOICES

Since the Art Nouveau period, Greenwich Village has been one big 'village of genius' and home of the artistic avant-garde. The radical paper *Masses*, whose contributors included Maxim Gorki, Bertrand Russell, and John Reed, had its offices here. In 1914, Gertrude Vanderbilt Whitney opened a gallery and provided a platform for contemporary artists, much of whose work was highly controversial. In 1916, members of the Playwrights' Theater settled on MacDougal Street and soon achieved fame, Eugene O'Neill among them.

After World War II the Bohemian image of 'the Village' persisted. In the 1950s, the beatnik movement flowered (Jack Kerouac and Allen Ginsberg); in the 1960s and early '70s the area was home to hippies and anti-Vietnam war activists (Abbie Hoffman and Jerry Rubin).

Chilling out on the High Line

New York's wealthiest families. It is one of the few museums that is dedicated solely to American art and that seeks out works from alternative media, such as film and video. By focusing its collection on contemporary American artists (both those of Ms. Whitney's era and those of today), it has gone a long way toward changing attitudes about the diversity and strength of the country's art. The permanent collection includes works by such artists as Andy Warhol, Alexander Calder, Georgia O'Keefe, Jackson Pollock, Jasper Johns, and Mark Rothko. Curators continue to build and show works by living artists.

The neighborhood between 14th and 39th streets, west of Sixth Avenue, is thriving after many years of decline. This is one of the trendiest gay neighborhoods in Manhattan. Stroll up Eighth Avenue, where you'll find gay bars and boutiques, as well as all sorts of restaurants. The **Joyce Theater** (www.joyce.org), at 19th Street, is one of the city's main modern dance venues. On 23rd Street, between Seventh and Eighth avenues, sits the famous (and infamous) **Chelsea Hotel**, with its distinctive wrought iron balconies. The former home to artists, rock stars and assorted sketchy characters, it is expected to reopen in 2019 following extensive renovation. Along the Hudson River, the Chelsea Piers (www.chelseapiers.com) serves up six blocks of sports and entertainment from 17th to 23rd streets.

Seventh Avenue is quieter, but you will still find many restaurants and stores. Loehmann's, on Seventh Avenue at 16th Street, is a prime source for discounted designer clothing. Sixth Avenue from 18th to 23rd streets was once known as the 'Ladies Mile.' For many years, the massive storefronts stood derelict; now they are inhabited by box stores like Old Navy and Bed, Bath, and Beyond.

Chelsea has long superseded SoHo as the place for **contemporary art**. There are close to 200 galleries on the far west side between Tenth and Twelfth avenues.

EXCURSIONS TO THE OUTER BOROUGHS

BROOKLYN

Brooklyn, which actually has a larger population than Manhattan, is one of America's largest urban centers. It is well worth a trip over the East River. **Brooklyn Heights**, the neighborhood closest to Manhattan, is easy to reach. Take subway lines 2 or 3 to Clark Street, or cross the Brooklyn Bridge on foot from the east side of City Hall Park (see page 33); the view is unparalleled.

Rising above the East River, the Heights is an attractive area of 19th-century brownstones and picturesque streets, long popular with writers and artists. The **Promenade** (three blocks down Clark Street from the bridge) is an esplanade with an impressive view, including both the Manhattan skyline and the Statue of Liberty. Late afternoon is a good time to go, when the towers of Lower Manhattan start to glow in the light of the setting sun. At the end of the Promenade, walk south along shady Hicks Street, in a quarter that has changed little since 1860.

If you are interested in subways and how they are run, then a trip to the **New York Transit Museum** is in order (www.

Waterfall in Brooklyn Botanic Garden

nytransitmuseum.org; Tue–Fri 10am–4pm, Sat–Sun 11am–5pm). Housed in an authentic 1930s subway station at the corner of Boerum Place and Schermerhorn Street, the museum has a great variety of exhibits, many with interactive components. They also have an annex museum in Grand Central Terminal (see page 45).

The **Brooklyn Museum of Art** ㉞ (www.brooklynmuseum.org; 200 Eastern Parkway; Wed–Sun 11am–6pm, Thu until 10pm, with exceptions) is the second-largest museum in New York, with exceptional collections of Egyptian, Asian, Persian, and pre-Columbian art. The permanent collection includes more than 1.5 million objects, and the African art collection is one of the largest and most important in the United States. Take the 2 or 3 subway to Eastern Parkway-Brooklyn Museum.

Adjacent to the museum is the **Brooklyn Botanic Garden**. Not to be confused with the larger New York Botanical Garden in the Bronx, it is nevertheless a peaceful place to stroll. Nearby is **Prospect Park**, a 526-acre (212-hectare) urban oasis designed by Frederick Law Olmsted and Calvert Vaux (who designed Central Park). A combined visit to the museum, botanic garden, and park is a nice way to spend a day.

THE BRONX

For a while now, the **Bronx** has had a reputation for crime and urban decay. While there are certainly parts of the Bronx where this is still true, visitors who haven't been here lately will be surprised. Several attractions make it worth a special trip to New York's only borough on the US mainland.

One such attraction is the **Bronx Zoo** ❸❺ (www.bronxzoo.com; Apr–Oct Mon–Fri 10am–5pm, Sat–Sun 10am–5.30pm, Nov–Mar daily 10am–4.30pm). At its most inviting from May through October, when all of the sections are open, the zoo has over 4,000 animals from almost 600 species. At the Congo Gorilla Forest you get to meet the zoo's gorillas up close. Though they are behind glass, there is still a lot of interaction with the crowd. Other popular exhibits are the Wild Asia monorail (where you can see tigers), JungleWorld, the World of Birds, Children's Zoo, the 4-D Theater, and, in the

Siberian tiger at the Bronx Zoo

summer, the Butterfly Garden. There is an extra fee for entry into most of these special rides and attractions, or you can purchase a Total Experience ticket that will give you access to everything.

To get to the zoo, take the 2 or 5 subway to East Tremont/West Farms Square. When you exit at street level, walk straight ahead (follow train uptown) for two and a half blocks on Boston Road to the zoo's Asia gate entrance (Gate A). Alternatively, you can take Metro North from Grand Central to Fordham station, then catch the BX9 bus to the Southern Boulevard Entrance. You can also take the BXM11 Express Bus from Midtown, which runs up Madison Avenue. The Bronx Zoo is the first stop after 99th Street.

Adjacent to the zoo is the 250-acre (100-hectare) **New York Botanical Garden** (www.nybg.org; Tue–Sun 10am–6pm, closes at 5pm in winter, with exceptions). Highlights include specialty gardens, an orchid collection, a 40-acre (16-hectare) uncut, almost virgin forest, and the Enid A. Haupt Conservatory. Children will enjoy learning about plants and nature in the adventure garden. The visitor center includes a shop, café, and visitor orientation area. To get there, take Metro North from Grand Central to the New York Botanical Garden stop.

QUEENS

The most diverse borough of the five that make up New York, Queens has several attractions of interest. During the silent

Yankee tours

Baseball fans may be interested to know that you can take a 60-min tour of Yankee Stadium, in the Bronx, during baseball season (May–September), but this is only permitted on days when the team is not playing at home. You must make an advance ticket reservation through Ticketmaster (tel: 800-745 3000; www.ticketmaster.com) or visit www.mlb.com.

movie era, Queens was the equivalent of today's Hollywood – the center of the motion-picture industry – and movies and TV shows are still made at the Kaufman Astoria Studios here. Located in the studio complex, on 35th Avenue at 36th Street in Astoria, the **American Museum of the Moving Image** (www.movingimage.us; Wed–Thu 10.30am–5pm, Fri 10.30am–8pm, Sat–Sun 10.30am–6pm) celebrates

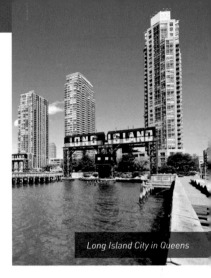

Long Island City in Queens

this early movie history and explores the art, technique, and technology of film, television, and digital media, examining their impact on society. To reach the museum, take the R subway to Steinway Street or the N to 36 Avenue (Astoria) and walk.

In Long Island City, just across from midtown Manhattan, is the **MoMA PS1** (22–25 Jackson Avenue at 46th Street; http://momaps1.org; Thu–Mon noon–6pm), the largest contemporary art museum in New York and well worth a visit. It's the second location of the Museum of Modern Art, beside midtown Manhattan. To get there, take the E subway to Court Square/23rd Street or the 7 to 45th Road/Courthouse Square.

Also in Long Island City is the **Noguchi Museum** ❸❻ (9-01 33rd Road, at Vernon Boulevard; www.noguchi.org; Wed–Fri 10am–5pm, Sat–Sun 11am–6pm), created by Japanese-American sculptor Isamu Noguchi to house a comprehensive collection of his works.

A shopkeeper presides over
traditional foodstuffs in Chinatown

WHAT TO DO

SHOPPING

If you can't afford to buy, you can always window-shop, a pastime in itself. Virtually anything is available in Manhattan for a price, which is sometimes, though certainly not always, a bargain.

WHEN AND WHERE TO SHOP

If you are looking for inexpensive New York souvenirs, avoid Midtown and the areas around major tourist attractions, such as the Empire State Building. Instead, try 14th Street, particularly between Fifth and Sixth avenues, as well as Chinatown, especially the north side of Canal and the blocks on either side of Mulberry. Greenwich Village can still be an interesting place to shop; browse the quirky smaller stores along Bleecker Street. SoHo, a major weekend destination for area shoppers, is the home of a few fine art galleries and plenty of designer-clothing and home-furnishings stores. There are also boutiques in Chelsea, and an eclectic variety of retailers in the East Village.

The reliable shopping neighborhoods have always been Fifth Avenue above 50th Street and Madison Avenue from Midtown to the Upper East Side. For decades the former was very chic, but is now increasingly predictable and loaded with chain and theme stores; the latter is home to some luxurious, high-end shops. The Upper West Side's shopping destination is the **Time Warner Center** overlooking Central Park, where more than 40 high-end retailers take up four floors at the base of the building on Columbus Circle.

WHAT TO BUY

Art and antiques. Art galleries and antiques shops are found throughout the city. The largest concentrations are along East 57th Street and up Madison Avenue to 84th Street. A movement away from SoHo, where there are still some galleries, has led to a boom in west Chelsea. There are some good antique stores on Bleecker Street, west of Christopher Street in Greenwich Village, as well as clustered around 10th and 11th streets at University Place. One institution worth visiting for its wide range of choices is the **Manhattan Art and Antiques Center** (1050 Second Avenue at 56th Street; www.the-maac.com), which boasts some 100 galleries selling ceramics, crystal, and assorted bric-a-brac.

Chelsea is the place to go for good flea markets, both open-air and enclosed. Try the **Hell's Kitchen Flea Market** (39th Street between Ninth and Tenth avenues; www.annexmarkets.com), with even more vendors, including many selling vintage clothing and jewelry or the **Chelsea Flea Market** (Uptown side of West 29th Street between Broadway and Sixth Avenue, Sat–Sun 6.30am–6pm) featuring up to 135 vendors selling antiques, collectibles, decorative arts, vintage clothing and jewelry.

Clothing. You really can find bargains among the prodigious array of clothes in the department stores, especially during end-of-season sales. But it would be a shame to limit your search to the bigger stores. Head to Madison Avenue above 60th Street for high-fashion boutiques; to SoHo (expensive) and the East Village (less expensive) for more daring designs; to Fifth Avenue for reliable luxury labels; and to the Meatpacking District

Macy's, the giant

Macy's, established in New York City in 1858, is the world's largest store, at 2.1 million sq ft (189,000 sq m). It stocks more than 500,000 items.

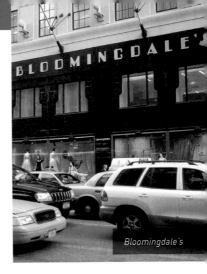
Bloomingdale's

for hip party-wear. The best place for discount designer clothing is **Century 21** (22 Cortlandt Street, between Broadway and Church and 1972 Broadway at 66th Street); almost everything starts at half price, and sometimes there are real bargains.

Computers and electronics. Approach the so-called 'discount' electronics stores of Midtown with a critical eye; sales techniques can be high-pressure and the prices are not always as good as you might think. Many of the dealers are reputable, however, and real bargains can be found if you know what you are looking for. New Yorkers shop at **Best Buy** (1280 Lexington Avenue; www.best buy.com) or **B&H Photo** (420 Ninth Avenue at 34th Street; www. bhphotovideo.com), where you can find absolutely everything and the staff are knowledgeable. Computer stores are concentrated on Fifth Avenue, above 20th Street; they include the **Apple Store** at 767 Fifth Avenue (see page 42).

Department stores. Macy's (34th and Broadway) and **Bloomingdale's** (59th and Lexington, and the SoHo location, at 504 Broadway) have everything; **Lord and Taylor** (38th and Fifth Avenue) is a little smaller. **Barney's** (61st and Madison) is known for cutting-edge fashion and upscale home furnishings. **Saks Fifth Avenue** (at 50th) is strictly high fashion for ladies who lunch and their gentlemen, as is **Bergdorf Goodman** (57th and Fifth Avenue).

Jewelry. Hit the Diamond District on West 47th for all prices and styles, but not always bargains; Fifth Avenue above 50th Street is the location for the high-end jewelers (Cartier, Tiffany, Harry Winston, Bulgari, Van Cleef and Arpels). Small boutiques in SoHo, Greenwich Village, and the East Village are good for hand-made originals.

Music and books. With the advent of online retailing, the big record stores have shut down. The city does still have some small, independent music stores with dedicated music lovers who keep them going, like **Other Music** (15 East 4th Street; www.othermusic.com) and **Bleecker Street Records** (239 Bleecker Street at Carmine Street; www.bleeckerstreetrecordsnyc.com).

In the book realm, **Barnes and Noble** has superstores catering to the masses (Warren and Greenwich streets, Union Square North, Lexington at 86th Street, and three more locations). A fixture on the independent bookstore scene is the excellent

⊙ MUSEUM SHOPS

American Folk Art Museum. 2 Lincoln Square; www.folkart museum.org. Rural crafts and toys from around the country.

Metropolitan Museum of Art Gift Shop. In the museum on Fifth Avenue and also at Rockefeller Center at 15 West 49th Street; http://store.metmuseum.org. Art books, posters, jewelry, reproductions.

The MoMA Design Store. 18 Spring Street, 11 West 53rd Street and 44 West 53rd Street; www.momastore.org. Designer furniture and household articles (see page 44).

The Museum of the City of New York. Fifth Avenue at 103rd Street; www.mcny.org. The place to go to find old prints of the city.

McNally Jackson (52 Prince Street at Mulberry; www.mcnallyjackson.com) in Nolita. Specialty bookstores all over the city cater to such tastes as theater (**Drama Book Shop** at 250 West 40th; www.dramabookshop.com), mysteries (**The Mysterious Bookshop** on Warren Street; www.mysteriousbookshop.com), science fiction and comics (**Forbidden Planet** on Broadway at 13th Street; www.fpnyc.com), and art

Strand Book Store

(MoMA or any museum store). Young readers will love Books of Wonder (18th Street west of Fifth Avenue; www.booksofwonder.com). For used books and out-of-print titles, head for **Strand Book Store** (Broadway at 12th Street; www.strandbooks.com). **New York originals. Zabar's** (Broadway between 80th and 81st; www.zabars.com) and **Dean & DeLuca** (560 Broadway in SoHo; www.deandeluca.com) are fancy-food heavens. Folks come from all over the world to shop at **Paper Source** (75 Fifth Avenue). Honestly, if **M&J Buttons** (Sixth Avenue between 37th and 38th; www.mjtrim.com) doesn't have the one you're looking for, it probably doesn't exist.

ENTERTAINMENT

They don't call New York the city that never sleeps for nothing. Whether you are interested in theater, the performing arts, a hot dance club, or just a quiet drink, you will have plenty of opportunities to have fun once the sun goes down. There is no way to cover the entire New York nightlife scene in these few pages. Luckily, there are plenty of resources for finding out what's going on either before you go, or once you have arrived in New York. The best places to find out what's going on are the Friday or Sunday *New York Times* (for mainstream events; www.nytimes.com), *The New Yorker or New York* magazines (good for arts and more sophisticated clubs and bars; www. newyorker.com and www.nymag.com), the *Village Voice* (an alternative online magazine, especially strong on music; www. villagevoice.com), or *Time Out New York* (a weekly magazine with wide coverage).

Tickets to most events can be purchased from Ticketmaster (tel: 800-745 3000 or www.ticketmaster.com), which charges a hefty service charge on top of the cost of the ticket itself. However,

⊘ DISCOUNT THEATER TICKETS

Discount theater tickets (up to 50 percent off) for same-day performances can be purchased at three TKTS locations in Manhattan (www.tdf.org/nyc/7/TKTS-ticket-booths). The most popular is in Father Duffy Square at 47th Street, which sells evening tickets daily after 3pm (2pm on Tue) and matinee tickets after 10am on Wed, Thu and Sat and after 11am on Sun. The other location is at South Street Seaport; it is open Mon–Sat 11am–6pm, Sun 11am–4pm (here matinee tickets are sold the day before the performance, and lines are usually shorter than in Times Square) and at Lincoln Center. There is also a fourth booth in Brooklyn (see website for details). All of them accept credit cards, cash, travelers' checks, or TKTS gift certificates.

it is possible to purchase same-day tickets for Broadway and off-Broadway musicals and plays at substantial discounts.

THEATER

One of the most popular activities for visitors is to take in a **Broadway** or **off-Broadway** show. Broadway theaters are concentrated in the Times Square area, but smaller off-Broadway houses are located all over town. Tickets for current

Theater in the West Village

hits must be booked ahead, sometimes months ahead. Curtain times are generally 8pm for evening performances, 2pm for matinees, which are usually on Wednesday, Saturday, and Sunday. Be prepared for a shock; the top shows charge over $100 for their best seats, and American theaters often do not follow the lead of other countries by charging much less for the less desirable seats.

CLASSICAL MUSIC AND DANCE

New York has a particularly vibrant and diverse music scene, offering every kind of style imaginable, from opera and classical music to jazz, pop, blues, country, world, and reggae. Admission to many concerts is free: the summer concerts in Central Park, for instance, or the lunch-time concerts held in the Financial District and midtown.

New York City's two major opera companies are the **Metropolitan Opera** and the **New York City Opera** (www.metopera.

Taxis in Times Square

org and www.nycopera. com). The Met performs at Lincoln Center, while the City Opera performs at different venues around town. If you want to see world-famous artists, go to the Met, but the City Opera also produces some fine work. As for classical music concerts, you are likely to find a dozen or so scheduled for a single evening; often at **Carnegie Hall** (57th Street and Seventh Avenue; www. carnegiehall.org).

You will have more chances to see good dance performances in New York than in almost any other city in the world; from the **American Ballet Theater** and **New York City Ballet** (both at Lincoln Center; www.abt.org and www.nycballet.com), to modern dance companies, many of which present their seasons at the **Joyce Theater** on Eighth Avenue (at 19th Street; www.joyce. org) and at **City Center** on Seventh Avenue (at 55th Street; www. nycitycenter.org). One should not forget such notable companies as those of Alvin Ailey (www.alvinailey.org), the Dance Theater of Harlem (www.dancetheatreofharlem.org), Merce Cunningham (http://mercecunningham.org), Mark Morris (http://markmorris dancegroup.org), and Paul Taylor (http://ptamd.org).

FILM

There are hundreds of mainstream movie screens in New York, but you will also have the chance to see many films that might not make it to your local multiplex. **MoMA**, the **Walter Reade Theater** at Lincoln Center, **Anthology Film Archive in the East Village** (http://anthologyfilmarchives.org), and the **Museum of the Moving Image** (www.movingimage.us) in Queens all have ongoing film series, mostly revivals of classic and art films. Other places to find movies that you might not otherwise see are: **Film Forum** (209 West Houston, between Sixth Avenue and Varick; www.filmforum.org); **New Plaza Cinema** (Broadway between 62nd and 63rd, https://newplazacinema.com); the **Quad Cinema** (34 West 13th Street, between Fifth and Sixth avenues; www.quadcinema.com); **Landmark Cinema** (657 West 57th Street at 12th Avenue; www.landmarktheatres.com); and the **Angelika Film Center** (Houston and Mercer streets).

DANCE CLUBS

The thing to keep in mind about dance clubs in New York is that clubs can be quite different depending on when and where you go. Among the hundreds of ever-changing venues (and themes), you might consider trendy (**Marquee**, 289 Tenth Avenue between 26th and 27th; www.marqueeny.com) or house (**Cielo**, 18 Little West 12th Street; www.cieloclub.com). There is also always the unapologetically chintzy megaclub **Webster Hall** (125 East 11th Street; www.websterhall.com).

CABARETS AND JAZZ CLUBS

New York is perhaps the center of world jazz. Listen to Jazz at **Iridium** (1650 Broadway at 51st Street; www.theiridium.com), the **Village Vanguard** (178 Seventh Avenue South; www.villagevanguard.com), the Blue Note (131 West 3rd Street; www.bluenotejazz.com/newyork), or **Birdland** (315 West 44th Street; www.birdlandjazz.com). Some other places where you can hear good music while you drink and/or dine include the **Metropolitan Room**

Serving cocktails at the Brass Monkey Bar

(34 West 22nd Street; www.metropolitanroom.com), **Joe's Pub** (in the Public Theater, Lafayette Street at Astor Place; http://joespub.publictheater.org), or **Café Carlyle** (35 East 76th Street; www.cafecarlylenewyork.com).

BARS

Hotel bars can be pretty swanky in New York. You will find popular ones at the **Shoreham**, **Mansfield**, **Baccarat**, and **Standard** hotels. The lobby bars at the **Royalton** and **Four Seasons** hotels are fashionable places to meet. **Monkey Bar** at the **Hotel Elysée** (60 East 54th Street; www.elyseehotel.com) and the **Paramount Bar & Grill** in the **Paramount Hotel** (235 West 46th Street; www.nycparamount.com) are old standbys.

Venture to the East Village, and you will find a good variety of bars: old-fashioned (**McSorley's Old Ale House** at 15 East 7th Street; https://mcsorleysoldalehouse.nyc), relaxed (**Von** at 3 Bleecker Street; www.vonbar.com), underground (**Raines Law Room** at 48 West 17th Street; www.raineslawroom.com), and fun (**Otto's Shrunken Head** at 538 East 14th Street; www.ottosshrunkenhead.com). Greenwich Village and the West Village offer a full range, from the cocktail oasis (**Little Branch** at 20 Seventh Avenue South at St Luke's Place) to the cozy beer-lovers' bar (**Blind Tiger Ale House** at 281 Bleecker Street at Jones Street; www.blindtigeralehouse.com) to the speakeasy-esque

(**Employees Only** at 510 Hudson Street; www.employeesonlynyc. com). Chelsea offers the whole gamut from gay with sports (**Gym** at 167 Eighth Avenue; www.gymsportsbar.com) to gay without attitude (**Barracuda** at 275 West 22nd Street).

Then there are bars for everyone, such as the **Brass Monkey Bar** in the Meatpacking District (55 Little West 12th Street; www. brassmonkeynyc.com), a large but relaxing place to enjoy a beer. Tried-and-true choices for impromptu celebrations with friends include the **Old Town Bar** (45 East 18th Street; www.oldtownbar. com) for a classic New York tavern experience.

SPORTS

WATCHING SPORTS

Baseball season is from April through September, and NYC has two major-league teams. The **Mets** play at Citi Field Stadium in Queens (take the 7 subway right to the stadium), and the **Yankees** play in the Bronx (the 4 and D subway lines stop at the stadium). You can usually buy tickets online at http://mlb.com and sometimes at the stadium on game day.

Football season runs September to January. The **Jets** and the **Giants**, New York City's professional football teams, both play nearby in New Jersey's Meadowlands at MetLife Stadium (there's shuttle-bus service from the Port Authority and a train from Penn Station). Basketball season runs October to April. The **New York Knicks** play at Madison Square Garden at 33rd Street and Seventh Avenue and the Brooklyn Nets play at the Barclay's Center at Atlantic and Flatbush avenues.

Tickets for football and basketball are hard to come by, but you can try www.stubhub.com, where fans sell tickets they cannot use. Hockey season generally runs from October to April; the

New York team is the **Rangers**, and they play at Madison Square Garden as well. The **US Open Tennis championships** are played at the US Tennis Center in Queens (7 subway to Mets-Willets Point) in late August and early September.

PLAYING SPORTS

Chances are, you didn't come to New York for the great out-doors. But when New Yorkers want to be active they go to **Central Park,** where you can rent a bicycle or a boat (both near the Loeb Boathouse, mid-Park near the Bethesda Terrace), or ice skate in winter (at **Wollman Rink,** mid-Park at 63rd, or **Lasker Rink,** 110th and Lenox Avenue). Otherwise, just follow the example of the many New Yorkers who jog, bike, and skate in Central Park and along the paths that line Hudson River Park. **Bowlmor Lanes** (110 University Place; www.bowlmor. com) in Greenwich Village has 42 bowling lanes and a carnival-themed club upstairs.

☉ NEW YORK FROM THE WATER

For children and adults, seeing Manhattan from the water is an experience not to be missed. There are great views from the Statue of Liberty and Staten Island ferries (see page 28). In addition, **Circle Line Cruises** (tel: 212-563 3200; www.circleline.com) offers various options, including a 2.5-hour Best of NYC Cruise, the 1.5-hour Landmarks Cruise, and the sunset Harbor Lights Cruise. Cruises leave from Pier 83 at 42nd Street and Twelfth Avenue. On Pier 62 at 22nd Street, Classic Harbor Line (tel: 212-627 1825; www.sail-nyc.com) provides sunset sails aboard their schooners *Adirondack* and America, as well as dinner, jazz, and wine-tasting cruises on their mini-yacht Manhattan.

Chelsea Piers (23rd Street at the Hudson River) is the one all-purpose destination for all your sporting needs. You will find facilities for virtually every sport imaginable, including skating, horseback riding, and swimming. For a complete run-down, tel: 212-336 6666 or http://venues.chelsea piers.com.

CHILDREN'S NEW YORK

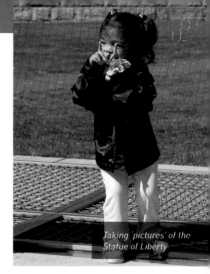

Taking 'pictures' of the Statue of Liberty

Central Park offers the greatest number of attractions including the Central Park Zoo and the Carousel. **Madison Square Park** (25th and Madison Avenue) and **Hudson River Park Playground** (Pier 51, Gansevoort Street and Hudson River) are favourites.

Almost all of New York's museums have exciting offerings for kids; some are devoted entirely to children. At the **Children's Museum of Manhattan** (212 West 83rd Street; www.cmom.org; Mon–Sun 10am–5pm, Sat until 7pm) kids can design their own subway mosaic art, build their own amusement park, or climb a giant Trojan horse while learning about ancient Greece.

For children's theatre try the **New Victory Theater** (www. newvictory.org), which makes an effort to present exciting and engaging performances a stone's throw from Times Square.

Many bookstores, including the large chains, have children's story hours. Books of Wonder (18 West 18th Street) is the city's oldest and largest independent children's bookstore.

CALENDAR OF EVENTS

January: Chinese New Year parades and celebrations (Chinatown, Mott, Mulberry and Bayard Streets), late January to mid-February. New York Boat Show.

March: St Patrick's Day Parade (Fifth Avenue) on March 17. Whitney Biennial (in even years, Whitney Museum of American Art).

April: Cherry Blossom Festival (Sakura Matsuri; Brooklyn Botanic Garden), late April–early May. Tribeca Film Festival (various locations), late April.

May: Ninth Avenue International Food Festival (9th Avenue/37th to 57th streets), early to mid-May. Fleet Week, late May.

June: Gay and Lesbian Pride Day Parade (Fifth Avenue & West Village), usually last Sunday in June. Museum Mile Festival (Fifth Avenue/82nd and 105th Streets), usually 2nd Tuesday in June. SummerStage (Central Park), June through September. Midsummer Night's Swing (Lincoln Center), late-June–July. Shakespeare in the Park (The Delacorte Theater in Central Park), June through August.

July: Macy's Fourth of July Fireworks (Hudson River), July 4th.

August: Harlem Week (venues throughout Harlem), throughout August. US Open Tennis Championship (Flushing Meadows, Queens), late August–early September.

September: Feast of San Gennaro (Little Italy), late September. 9/11 Commemorations on September 11. New York Film Festival (Lincoln Center venues), late September to early October.

October: Halloween Parade (Greenwich Village, Sixth Avenue/Spring and 23rd Streets), October 31.

November: New York City Marathon (throughout city), 1st Sunday in November. Macy's Thanksgiving Day Parade (77th Street and Central Park to Broadway and 34th Street), Thanksgiving Day. Radio City Music Hall Christmas Spectacular (Radio City Music Hall), throughout November and December.

December: Christmas Tree Lighting (Rockefeller Center), late November/early December. New Year's Eve (Times Square), December 31.

EATING OUT

In a city with more than 26,000 restaurants, New Yorkers dine out a lot. You'll find some of the best restaurants in the country in New York, and some are quite expensive, but you won't have to take out a second mortgage on your home to eat well in this city either – even in Manhattan. The variety of restaurants and eating options is unsurpassed. You can enjoy Indian dosas from a street vendor, dine at the latest celebrity chef's restaurant, or simply enjoy a really great meal at a favorite neighborhood spot.

PRICE

You can eat incredibly well in New York for an average amount of money. Dinner (including one drink and tip) generally costs around $50 per person. A good way to experience some of the best (and often most expensive) restaurants, without blowing your budget, is to drop in for lunch instead of dinner. The lunch menu is almost always cheaper. For example, a two-course lunch at Jean-Georges (see page 54) costs $68; a three-course dinner menu starts at $148, even though the quality and variety of the offerings are similar. Prix-fixe meals, particularly pre-theater dinners (usually served 6–7pm) are vastly cheaper than the à la carte menu and are being offered with increasing frequency. If food is the focus of your trip, then plan your visit around one of the seasonal 'NYC Restaurant Weeks,' when more than 380 top-end restaurants offer bargain two-course prix fixe lunches (around $26) and three-course dinners (around $42).

MEALS AND MEAL TIMES

Breakfast is usually served from 7am through at least 9am. Brunch is usually just on weekends, 11am–3pm. Lunch is generally noon–2pm. Dinner is served anywhere from 5.30pm until 11pm, or later in some places. New Yorkers tend to eat dinner a bit later than elsewhere in the US and you will find restaurants busiest between 7pm and 9pm.

NEW YORK SPECIALTIES

Iconic delis and the pastrami sandwich

Pastrami with mustard on rye: the quintessential New York sandwich. Delis all over the United States lay claim to a New York-style pastrami sandwich, but the best are served in authentic New York delicatessens, where you will pay around $15 for a sandwich. Pastrami starts first with beef brisket cured in brine, which is then smoked to give it its unique flavor. It is sliced thick or thin (usually your choice) and served with mustard on rye for a tender and juicy melt-in-your-mouth sandwich.

Early immigrants brought the Eastern European tradition of salted and cured meats to New York. Katz's Delicatessen in the lower East Side opened in 1888 and was immortalized in the famous deli scene in the film *When Harry Met Sally*. During the heyday of New York's leading delis, struggling actors rubbed shoulders at the counters with celebrities, presidents, and New

⊘ RESTAURANT GUIDE

The Zagat Survey of New York City Restaurants is one of the best reference guides for dining out in New York City. Published annually, the guide solicits local diners (in New York this is a large, avid, and opinionated group) to produce a fairly comprehensive and informative compendium. All the information is also available online at: www.zagat.com.

York movers and shakers. Those days may have passed, but it's not too late to visit one of these iconic delis: **Mile End Deli** (53 Bond NoHo in Manhattan and 97A Hyt Boerum Hill in Brooklyn; www.mileenddeli.com); **The Carnegie** (4 Pennsylvania Plaza, tel: 212-757 2245; www.carnegiedeli.com); **Katz's** (205 East Houston at Ludlow, tel: 212-254 2246; www.katzsdelicatessen.com); and **2nd Ave. Deli** (162 East

The pastrami sandwich – a New York institution

33rd Street between Lexington and Third avenues, tel: 212-689 9000; www.2ndavedeli.com).

Diners and coffee shops

You will find diners and coffee shops dotted around every neighborhood of New York, usually with vast menus and reasonable prices. The diner immortalized in the sitcom *Seinfeld* is **Tom's Restaurant** (2880 Broadway at 112th Street; www.tomsrestaurant.net), but it's only the front that you'll recognize.

Bakeries

The city's neighborhoods have some lovely local bakeries. They are great places to pick up a sandwich, breakfast pastry, or sweet cupcake treat. **Once Upon a Tart** (135 Sullivan Street; www.onceuponatart.com), in SoHo, offers tarts, sandwiches, scones, and other treats, which you can grab to go, or eat at one of the outdoor tables while watching the SoHo scene. **Le Pain Quotidien** (locations throughout Manhattan; www.lepainquotidien.com) is a Belgian chain where you can sit at communal tables and enjoy delicious fresh bread, tarts, and pastries. Francophiles should also pay a visit to **Maison Ladurée** (at 864 Madison Ave; www.laduree.fr) famous for its macarons which come in a variety of flavours, such as caramel, framboise, praline and cinnamon-raisin. With its antique upholstered chairs and vintage-style wallpaper, the interior resembles the original 156-year old patisserie.

Bagels

Bagels were allegedly invented in New York, and the best examples can still be found here. Aficionados argue over where to find the perfect bagel, but you won't go wrong with **Ess-a-Bagel** (831 Third Avenue; www.ess-a-bagel.com), **Murray's** (500 Avenue of the Americas; www.murraysbagels.com), or one of the many neighborhood bagel shops. All that can be said for certain is that bagels need to be fresh (no more than a few hours old), so stick to the shops that make their own. Add cream cheese, lox (smoked salmon) and a squeeze of lemon,

⊙ BRUNCH

If you are in New York over a weekend, then you should try to have Saturday or Sunday brunch. New Yorkers love lazy weekend brunches, which are served at most restaurants, usually starting at 11am (sometimes earlier) through late afternoon (3–4pm). Take the hefty Sunday *New York Times* with you and enjoy. Best to try to go earlier than noon if you don't want to wait. It is normal to see groups of people waiting patiently outside their favorite brunch spots. Diners also provide good brunch options.

and you have a great New York meal.

Pizza

New York is known for pizza, though as anyone who has ever bought a tepid slice from one of the city's pizzerias can tell you, it's not all of the best quality. However, there is infinite variety, from thin crust to thick and chewy to artisanal, oven-baked pizzas. **John's** (278 Bleecker Street; www.johnsbrickovenpizza.com) will

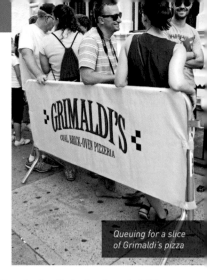

Queuing for a slice of Grimaldi's pizza

never do you wrong, though they don't sell single slices. In Little Italy, the clam pie is popular at **Lombardi's** (32 Spring Street; www.firstpizza.com). **Grimaldi's** (1 Front Street; www.grimaldis-pizza.com) in Brooklyn, at the foot of the Brooklyn Bridge, is a treat after a walk over the bridge. Several pizzerias use the name, but there's only one official **Patsy's**, an institution in Harlem since 1933 (2287 First Avenue; www.thepatsyspizza.com).

New York cheesecake

This is the classic, New York comfort food, available almost everywhere in many variations. A graham cracker crumb crust is topped with a rich, smooth cheesecake to make a delicious treat. The cheesecake at **Junior's** shouldn't be missed (Times Square, West 45th Street between Broadway and Eighth Avenue, or the original location in Brooklyn, 386 Flatbush Avenue Extension at Dekalb Avenue; www.juniorscheesecake.com).

The original Shake Shack in Madison Square Park

Steakhouses

Carnivores will delight in the almost 100 steakhouse options in New York. One of the best is **BLT Prime** (111 East 22nd Street; http://bltrestau rants.com); **Old Homestead** (56 Ninth Avenue; www.theoldhomestead steakhouse.com) is a classic; and **Peter Luger** (178 Broadway at Driggs Street; www.peterluger. com) in Williamsburg, Brooklyn, is often cited as the city's, if not the country's, best place for a porterhouse.

Burgers and hot dogs

The perfect budget meal, the hot dog makes you feel like a real New Yorker, whether you are grabbing one at Yankee Stadium or making a pit stop at a street cart after a night of dancing. The following are all good options: the quirky **Crif Dogs** (113 Saint Marks Place in the East Village; www.crifdogs.com) with its wide range of specialty dogs; the venerable **Papaya King** (179 East 86th Street; www.papayaking.com); and **Gray's Papaya** (2090 Broadway; www.grayspapayanyc.com).

   New burger joints seem to open all the time. You will find burgers served in restaurants in every price range, from the top restaurants to the popular Shake Shack chain. The following all serve highly rated burgers: the burger joint at **Le Parker Meridien** (119 West 56th Street between Sixth and

Seventh avenues; www.parkermeridien.com); **Rare Bar & Grill** (in Shelburne Murray Hill Hotel, 303 Lexington Avenue at 37th Street; in Hilton New York Fashion District, 152 West 26th Street between Sixth and Seventh avenues; www.rarebarandgrill.com); **Corner Bistro** (331 West 4th Street at Jane Street; www.cornerbistrony.com); and the **Shake Shack** (original outdoor stand in Madison Square Park, and other locations in Manhattan, Brooklyn, and Queens; www.shakeshack.com).

Carts

Some of the best food in New York is served on sidewalks – and it is not just hot dogs and pretzels. You can find Indian dosas, bratwurst, kebabs, steamed rolled rice noodles, and Mexican tamales. Many of the best vendors are located in the outer boroughs (Queens, in particular), but there is a fair share in Manhattan. Just look for the cart with the line and follow the New Yorkers. Many New Yorkers pick up their breakfast on the street from carts serving coffee, bagels, muffins, and breakfast pastries. A small coffee costs about $1, which is about as cheap as you will get.

Healthy fast food options

The following are all reliable, quick, relatively healthy, and inexpensive options while on the go. **Au Bon Pain** (www.aubonpain.com) is a bakery/café chain serving quality soups, salads, rice and pasta dishes, sandwiches, and pastries at many locations throughout the city. **Hale and Hearty Soups** (several locations in midtown; www.haleandhearty.com) serves soup that is well worth the price. **Whole Foods Market**, with seven locations throughout the city (www.wholefoodsmarket.com) is a chain of natural foods supermarkets with self-serve cafeterias and a wide variety of prepared foods.

ETHNIC ENCLAVES

Chinatown (see page 71) is the best-known locale for Chinese cuisine in New York, but less well publicized is Flushing, Queens, which has a number of excellent Chinese restaurants. You will find a group of Vietnamese restaurants on Baxter Street, Chinatown, not far from the US Courthouse.

Eating in Chinatown

Though **Little Italy** has shrunk to a couple of blocks of Mulberry Street north of Canal Street, there are still Italian restaurants that can pass muster; most of the places here will do if all you want is a plate of pasta and a glass of wine. Another group of Italian restaurants can be found on Bleecker Street between Thompson Street and Seventh Avenue.

Little India, on Sixth Street between First and Second avenues, has some very cheap Indian restaurants, only a handful of which are actually good (Panna II at 93 First Avenue, is one of the best; www.pannatwo.com).

The above are some of the most popular options, but you can find food from almost anywhere in the world: Brazilian restaurants can be found in a cluster on 45th and 46th streets in Midtown (between Sixth and Seventh avenues), and Korean eateries dot 32nd Street between Fifth Avenue and Broadway, while Egyptian places are concentrated over in Long Island City. For a multi-ethnic feast, investigate Ninth Avenue in the 40s and 50s.

PLACES TO EAT

We have used the following symbols to give an idea of the average price for a three-course meal for one, not including drinks or tip:

$$$$	50–100 dollars
$$$	35–50 dollars
$$	25–35 dollars
$	below 25 dollars

DOWNTOWN

Blue Hill $$$$ *75 Washington Place (at Washington Square West), tel: 212-539 1776; www.bluehillfarm.com*. One of New York's finest and most ecologically sustainable tables. Many of the incredibly fresh, and lovingly prepared, ingredients on the seasonal New American menu come from the restaurant's farm in the Hudson Valley.

Blue Water Grill $$$ *31 Union Square West (at 16th), tel: 212-675 9500; www.bluewatergrillnyc.com*. Housed in a spacious former bank, this popular Union Square seafood restaurant is consistently crowded. The raw offerings are especially good. The prices are on the high side of moderate, but still quite reasonable. Reservations are necessary unless you want to sit outside.

Cafeteria $$ *119 7th Avenue (at 17th), tel: 212-414 1717; www.cafeteria group.com*. One of Chelsea's trendy options, Cafeteria is open 24 hours and offers reconstructed bistro and diner food for hip club-goers. Where else will you be able to get pancakes or grilled salmon at 4.30am? Consistently good, if not overly exciting.

Eataly $$$ *200 5th Avenue (at 23rd), tel: 212-229 2560; www.eataly.com*. The brainchild of Mario Batali and the Bastianich family, this market and gourmet food court is always swarmed with folks sampling the imported Italian fare, from pizza, panini, and pasta, to espresso, beer and gelato. There are sit-down restaurants, bars and takeout stands; something for every taste and budget.

Eleven Madison Park $$$$ *11 Madison Avenue (at 24th), tel: 212-889 0905;* www.elevenmadisonpark.com. This restaurant keeps getting better and better. One of the most elegant dining rooms in the city, with ceilings that reach into the clouds, this Flatiron business lunch staple is also one of the best places for dinner, garnering three Michelin stars.

Gotham Bar and Grill $$$$ *12 East 12th Street (5th Avenue and University), tel: 212-620 4020;* www.gothambarandgrill.com. This large, airy space is usually filled with well-dressed downtowners who appreciate the exquisite food and well-chosen, but expensive wines. Few other upscale restaurants are as inviting to single diners, who can order and eat at the bar in comfort and style. The fixed-price restaurant week lunch is a great deal.

Gramercy Tavern $$$$ *42 E. 20th Street (between Broadway & Park), tel: 212-477 0777;* www.gramercytavern.com. Seasonally inspired fresh and local ingredients are the focus of this popular New American tavern with excellent service. Reservations are often difficult to come by, but you can also eat in the front tavern, which accepts walk-ins. Tasting menus available for lunch and dinner.

Hangawi $$$ *12 East 32nd Street (5th and Madison avenues), tel: 212-213 0077;* www.hangawirestaurant.com. Diners at this vegetarian Korean restaurant will quickly become suffused with a Zen-like calm. Discard your cares (and your shoes) at the door, and try mountain-root vegetables, porridges, and other delicacies.

Hill Country $$ *30 West 26th Street (at Broadway), tel: 212-255 4544;* www.hillcountry.com/nyc. This Texas barbecue near the Empire State Building is justly celebrated for its brisket, sausage and honky-tonk atmosphere. It is more expensive than a roadside stand, but from Tuesday through Saturday there are live music shows, most free to the public.

Il Buco $$$$ *47 Bond Street, tel: 212-533 1932;* www.ilbuco.com. An intimate place to sample hearty Italian and Mediterranean fare, this former antique shop fills up with couples and small parties who appreciate the rustic preparations of meat and pasta, the excellent wine list, and the cluttered, but cozy setting.

Kanoyama $$$$ *175 2nd Avenue (at 11th), tel: 212-777 5266;* www.kano
yama.com. East Village Japanese restaurant with a strong following.
The portions are generous and the fish is incredibly fresh. Friendly staff.

Momofuku Ssäm Bar $$$$ *207 2nd Avenue, tel: 212-254 3500;* www.
momofuku.com. An eccentric masterpiece and part of David Chang's
ever-expanding Momofuku empire. What started as a 'Korean burrito
bar' has become one of the city's hippest and most unpredictable tables,
serving innovative cuisine inspired by Korea, the American South, and
everywhere in between. If you have a hungry bunch, reserve a Bo Ssäm
meal, which involves an entire slow-cooked pork shoulder that is served
with rice, kimchee, and sauce and wrapped in pieces of bibb lettuce.
Other Momofuku restaurants are all worth a visit, including Noodle Bar,
Milk Bar, Nishi and the tiny, but wondrous Ko.

Nobu $$$$ *195 Broadway, tel: 212-219 0500;* www.noburestaurants.com.
Still wildly popular and trendy (forget Saturday night), Nobu continues
to pack in crowds with its innovative nouvelle Japanese menu. There
is another Nobu restaurant at 40 West 57th Street (tel: 212-757 3000).

Noodle Village $ *13 Mott Street (near Chatham Square), tel: 212-233 0788;*
www.noodlevillage.com. This Cantonese restaurant at the southern
end of Mott Street in Chinatown boasts that their chef arrived straight
from Hong Kong. They also proudly claim that there is no MSG added to
their dishes. The congee and noodle soups are popular choices. A great
cheap, healthy and fast option.

Nyonya $ *199 Grand Street (at Mulberry), tel: 212-334 3669;* www.
ilovenyonya.com. This is the place to go for an introduction to the
delicious and spicy cuisine of Malaysia. The Hainanese chicken is
good, but don't overlook spicy beef rendang or one of the equally
tasty seafood dishes.

Shabu-Tatsu $$ *216 East 10th Street (between 1st and 2nd avenues), tel:
212-477 2972;* www.shabutatsu.com. At this small, popular Japanese
restaurant, diners choose a selection of thinly sliced meats and vegeta-
bles for *shabu-shabu* (swirled in a hot pot of seasoned water), sukiyaki

(a Japanese stew), or yakiniku (cooked on a grill) and cook it themselves in the middle of the table.

Shanghai Cuisine $$ *89 Bayard Street (at Mulberry), tel: 212-732 8988;* www.shanghaicuisinenyc.com. Shanghai cuisine is more than just soup and dumplings, as this Chinatown spot proves. Fresh interpretations of traditional specialties, including smoked fish and mock duck, will reward the adventurous. Cash only.

Tamarind Tribeca $$$$ *99 Hudson Street (at Franklin Street), tel: 212-775 9000;* www.tamarindtribeca.com. There are plenty of mediocre Indian restaurants in the city, but this is an innovative and elegant take on the cuisine, leaps beyond the typical samosas and chicken tikka masala. The excellent four-course lunch is less than $30.

Union Square Café $$$$ *101 East 19th Street, tel: 212-243 4020;* www.unionsquarecafe.com. Gracious service and reliably good food are two reasons why this restaurant remains one of New York's perennial favorites. Although the Mediterranean-inspired cuisine is no longer cutting-edge, the food still dazzles in unexpected ways. Even the fried calamari, now a restaurant staple, is heads above the chewy appetizer most people have come to expect. The extensive and reasonably priced wine list is an added bonus.

MIDTOWN

Aquavit $$$$ *65 East 55th Street (at Madison and Park avenues), tel: 212-307 7311;* www.aquavit.org. Like the Scandinavian fare served here, the décor is modern, precise and minimally adorned. There is fish on the menu, of course, but also meatballs, squab and beef. Try a glass of the eponymous spirits.

Aureole Liberty Room $$$$ *One Bryant Park, 135 West 42nd Street (at Broadway and 6th Avenue), tel: 212-319 1660;* www.charliepalmer.com. This is arguably the best restaurant in the Times Square neighborhood. It is certainly the most expensive, but the lunch, pre-theater, and Sunday prix-fixe menus are great deals.

Becco $$$ *355 West 46th Street (8th and 9th avenues), tel: 212-397 7597;* www.becco-nyc.com. Come for the delicious pasta at this rustic Theater District favorite, which combines reasonable prices and high quality. The two-course fixed-price meal is particularly good value, especially since the pasta is an all-you-can-eat special.

Le Bernardin $$$$ *155 West 51st Street, tel: 212-554 1515;* www.le-bernardin.com. Eric Ripert has carved out his niche, and no one is complaining. Le Bernardin serves only seafood and only the city's best. Every item on the fixed-price menu is a winner, from the simplest pan-seared cod to a whole-roasted red snapper for two. Divinely inspired desserts. No lunch Sat. Closed Sun.

La Bonne Soupe $$ *48 West 55st Street, tel: 212-586 7650;* www.labonnesoupe.com. The line is always long at this reliable French bistro around the corner from MoMA, where they have been dishing out steak frites, quiche, omelettes, fondues, and excellent onion soup for 40 years.

Carmine's $$$ *200 West 44th Street (Broadway and 8th Avenue), tel: 212-221 3800;* www.carminesnyc.com. The huge portions of hearty Italian food at this Theater District mainstay are served family-style, so the prices aren't as high as they seem at first glance. Always mobbed and loud, but consistently churning out massive quantities of food at all hours, this is a reliable standby eatery.

Churrascaria Plataforma $$$$ *316 West 49th Street (8th and 9th avenues), tel: 212-245 0505;* www.plataformaonline.com. All-you-can eat Brazilian rodízios (huge meat-heavy buffet) make this one of the most popular and fun places to go when you are in the mood to eat, and eat a lot. Start at the salad bar, a healthy prelude to the parade of skewered meats, which doesn't stop until you're about to explode. A *caipirinha* cocktail will set your taste buds on the right track.

DB Bistro Moderne $$$$ *55 West 44th Street (between 5th and 6th avenues), tel: 212-391 2400;* www.dbbistro.com. Chef Daniel Boulud's bistro is awash in culinary surprises and Art Deco glitz, with a clientele to match. The burger is a modern classic, made with sirloin, short ribs, foie gras and black truffles.

Freds at Barney's $$$ *660 Madison Avenue, 9th floor (at 60th in Barney's), tel: 212-833 2200;* www.barneys.com/freds. This lunch spot in Barney's department store is wildly popular, and justifiably so. The antipasto plate is a real charmer, but the Madison Avenue chopped salad with Italian tuna and the more substantial options are also very good. Don't miss dessert. Dinner is also served, but only until 9pm at the latest.

The Grill $$$$ *99 East 52nd Street (between Lexington and Park avenues), tel: 212-375 9001;* www.thegrillnewyork.com. Located in the Seagram Building, chef Mario Carbone creates impeccable American specialties in this mid-century style chophouse. Prime aged steaks, including the classic porterhouse, lobster and duck are included in the variety of seafood and meat dishes available. Cocktails also remain classic with the Manhattan, champagne cocktail and a variety of martinis on the menu. Dinner only.

Sardi's $$$ *234 West 44th Street at Broadway and Eighth Ave, tel: 212-221 8440;* www.sardis.com. Of course, lunch and dinner are served at this legendary Theater District mainstay, but even if you're not drinking, a drink at the bar is a must. Sip a cocktail surrounded by the trademark caricatures of every Broadway name. Friendly barmen.

Smith and Wollensky $$$$ *49th Street (at 3rd Avenue), tel: 212-753 1530;* www.smithandwollensky.com. The well-aged steaks served in this male-dominated classic eaterie are consistently and perfectly grilled. The wine list is excellent, although expensive; sometimes shockingly so. The less expensive grill just around the corner is a good alternative for anyone without an expense account.

THE UPPER EAST SIDE

Café Boulud $$$$ *20 East 76th Street (near Madison Avenue, in the Surrey Hotel), tel: 212-772 2600;* www.cafeboulud.com. Daniel Boulud has mastered the art of casual elegance. Calling this a tarted-up bistro strikes a note of sacrilege, but the label can't detract from what a great chef can produce when he takes his gloves off.

Café Sabarsky $$$ *1048 5th Avenue (at 86th Street), tel: 212-288 0665; www.kurtgutenbrunner.com/restaurants/cafe-sabarsky.* Enter this wood-paneled salon within the Neue Galerie (see page 54), and you'll think you're on Vienna's Ringstrasse. Chef Kurt Gutenbrunner lives up to the surroundings, while museum food is taken to new heights by the beef goulash, Viennese sausage, linzer torte, and other fare from the banks of the Danube.

Candle Café $$ *1307 3rd Avenue (between 74th and 75th streets), tel: 212-472 0970; www.candlecafe.com.* The staff at this small bastion of health serve up clever and tasty vegan fare. Even carnivores might be tempted by the stir-fried tempeh with peanut sauce and casseroles of sweet potatoes and steamed greens, not to mention the desserts. Also at 2427 Broadway (between 89th and 90th Streets) and 54 East 79th Street.

The Loeb Boathouse $$$$ *Central Park, enter on East 72nd Street, tel: 212-517 2233; www.thecentralparkboathouse.com.* The lake and surrounding greenery of Central Park are the most memorable part of a meal in this airy, glass-fronted dining room and waterside terrace (the perfect spot for a warm-weather brunch). True to the watery surroundings, the kitchen sends out such nautically inspired flourishes as sea urchin and caviar in a scallop shell and pan-roasted monkfish and seared wild striped sea bass. Meanwhile, brunchtime hits of the French toast and omelette variety satisfy the hungry weekend crowds.

Sarabeth's $$$ *1295 Madison Avenue (at East 92nd Street), tel: 212-410 7335; www.sarabethsrestaurants.com.* Cheery and incredibly popular, Sarabeth's is best for its home-style breakfasts and brunch, from waffles to fluffy eggs, although succulent roasts and other serious and well-prepared dishes come out at dinnertime. Child-friendly environs and homey decor. There are four other locations: at 339 Greenwich Street, corner of Jay Street, tel: 212-966 0421; at 381 Park Avenue South, between 26th and 27th streets, tel: 212-335 0093; at 423 Amsterdam Avenue, between 80th and 81st streets, tel: 212-496 6280; and at 40 Central Park South, tel: 212-826 5959.

Sfoglia $$$$ *1402 Lexington Avenue (at 92nd Street), tel: 212-831 1402;* www.sfogliarestaurant.com. This New York branch of the original Nantucket restaurant is just as at home on the Upper East Side. An unobtrusive little trattoria, it offers seasonal Northern Italian country fare in a casual and intimate setting. Diners return for the inventive, frequently changing menu. There are only ten tables, so plan ahead for dinner reservations. The homemade bread is to die for.

The View $$$$ *1535 Broadway (at 45th and 46th streets), tel: 212-704 8900;* www.theviewnyc.com. High atop the Marriott Marquis Hotel in Times Square is New York's only revolving restaurant, with a wonderful panoramic view of the skyline.

THE UPPER WEST SIDE

Barney Greengrass $$ *541 Amsterdam Avenue (between 86th and 87th streets), tel: 212-724 4707;* www.barneygreengrass.com. The faded murals and formica tables are deceptively downbeat, but New Yorkers continue to herald this West Side institution as the best place in town for lox, smoked sturgeon, chopped liver, and other Jewish fare. Weekend lines are long, but in them you might spot Bill Murray, Woody Allen, and other celebrity regulars. Closed Monday.

Calle Ocho $$$ *45 West 81st Street, tel: 212-873 5025;* www.calleocho nyc.com. This fun and festive celebration of Latin flavors has found a home in the Excelsior Hotel. Sip sangria and mojitos, enjoy the music, and be wowed by the Cuban-inspired dishes for dinner, or better yet, for its always-hopping weekend brunch.

Jean-Georges $$$$ *1 Central Park West (at 60th and 61st streets, in the Trump International Hotel), tel: 212-299 3900;* www.jean-georges.com. Chef Jean-Georges Vongerichten's four-star experiment in ultra-chic surroundings is well worth the price. For the ultimate, try the seasonally focused tasting menu; for the experience of just being here, order the prix-fixe lunch at a fraction of the cost.

Kefi $$$ *222 West 79th Street, tel: 212-873 0200;* www.michaelpsilakis. com. This Greek restaurant opened quietly, until word of mouth about its affordable and spectacular takes on traditional classics turned it into a huge hit and its chef/owner Michael Psilakis into a star.

Shun Lee West $$$$ *43 West 65th Street (Columbus Avenue and Central Park West), tel: 212-595 8895;* www.shunleerestaurants.com. Those used to take-out noodles, fried rice, and General Tso's chicken will be amazed at how refined Chinese food can be. Attached to the original restaurant is the much less expensive Shun Lee Café.

Tessa $$$ *349 Amsterdam Avenue, tel: 212-390 1974;* www.tessanyc.com. A popular Mediterranean tavern combining French, Italian and Spanish cuisines, located close to Central Park and the Beacon Theater. Chef Nicholas McCann produces dishes based on locally sourced, fresh, pro- duce as well as speciality ingredients thus, the extensive menu changes seasonally. There is an extensive wine list to choose from offering wines from around the globe.

A–Z TRAVEL TIPS

A SUMMARY OF PRACTICAL INFORMATION

A

ACCOMMODATIONS (See also Youth hostels and YMCAs and the list of Recommended hotels)

It is increasingly hard to find a decent yet reasonably priced hotel room in New York. The average price of a hotel room in Manhattan is now about $250 per night. The high season is fall and winter, particularly from late November through New Year's Day, when rates can be as much as 25 percent higher; the low season is January through mid-March, though some hotels also reduce rates in the summer. Advance reservations are often crucial; the city is very crowded. Be aware that quoted rates will not include a sales tax of 14.75 percent, plus a $3.50 per day occupancy tax. Most hotels do not provide breakfast. At many hotels children can sleep in their parents' room at no extra charge.

You can also find bed and breakfasts in the city. However, their rates ($150–$300) can vary quite dramatically and can, in some cases, be higher than many hotel rates. It is a good option if you want to feel part of the city and at home in a neighborhood. Good websites to search: www.bnbfindor.com and www.bedandbreakfast.com. City Lights New York (www.citylightsnewyork.com) is a registry of carefully selected accommodations both hosted and unhosted.

AIRPORTS

New York is served by three major airports: **John F. Kennedy International** (JFK) and **Newark Liberty International** (EWR), the two international airports, and **LaGuardia** (LGA), mostly for domestic flights.

John F. Kennedy Airport (tel: 718-244 4444; www.jfkairport.com) is in Queens, about 15 miles (24km) southeast of midtown Manhattan. The JFK AirTrain (https://jfkairport.com/to-from-airport/air-train) is the cheapest way to get into town. It usually takes well over an hour, but operates every 7 to 12 minutes during peak times (4–7.30am and 3–8pm) and every 15 or 20 minutes during non-peak hours. Take the AirTrain (http://web.mta.info/mta/airtrain.htm) to Howard Beach or Jamaica stations ($5), where you can connect with A or E subway trains ($2.75) or the Long Island Rail Road (LIRR) to Penn Station. A taxi from the airport to any destination below 96th Street in Manhattan takes about 45 minutes to an hour, depending on traffic, and costs $52 flat rate, not including tolls, peak hours surcharge ($4.50) or tip. Shuttle buses cost around $20–25 per person. SuperShuttle (www.supershuttle.com) runs 24 hrs to any Manhattan destination and NYC Airporter (www.nycair porter.com) runs to Grand Central Terminal, Port Authority Bus Terminal and midtown hotels.

Newark Liberty Airport (tel: 973-961 6000; www.newarkairport.com) is located in New Jersey, 16 miles (26km) southwest of midtown Manhattan. Newark is usually more convenient than JFK for those staying in the Theater District. Taxis to Midtown take 30–45 minutes and metered fares usually run around $55, not including additions for tolls for the tunnels ($13 extra) and tip. Newark Airport Express (newarkairportexpress.com) shuttle costs about $17 (one way) per person to Grand Central Terminal, the Port Authority Bus Terminal on 42nd Street, or Bryant Park. AirTrain Newark (www.newarkairport.com/to-from-airport/air-train) takes you to Newark Liberty station, where you can take a NJ Transit commuter train to Penn Station (note these can be busy and are not equipped to handle large pieces of luggage). It operates every 3 minutes during peak times (5am–midnight), every 10 minutes during non-peak hours; NJ Transit commuter train schedules vary. The total cost is about $12.50.

LaGuardia Airport (tel: 718-533 3400; www.laguardiaairport.com) is located in Queens, 8 miles (13km) northeast of midtown Manhattan. Taxis to Midtown take 30–40 minutes depending on traffic and usually cost $30–$35, not including tolls or tip. SuperShuttle and NYC Airporter charge around $12–$16 for the trip. The trip by subway and bus can take considerably longer than a taxi but costs only $2.75 if you purchase a MetroCard. The M60 bus connects with the subways in Manhattan; Q70 Limited, Q47, Q72 and Q48 buses connect with the subway in Queens.

B

BUDGETING FOR YOUR TRIP

Hotel: For a double room (before tax), expect to pay over $150 per night for a budget room, up to $275 for a moderate room, up to $350 for an expensive room, and over $500 for a luxury room. The only way to spend less than $100 per night is to stay in a hostel or YMCA.

Meals: Breakfast can be had for $6–8; lunch costs from $8–10 for a sandwich and drink from a deli to $12–15 in an inexpensive restaurant; dinner can cost anywhere from $15 to $150 per person. A glass of wine is rarely less than $7, and a bottle is considered very cheap at $20.

Transportation: An unlimited MetroCard for one week costs $32.

Museums and attractions: Some museums and attractions are expensive ($25 for the Guggenheim), but those museums that belong to the city are technically only allowed to ask for a donation, so there you can pay as you wish. Many museums are free at least one evening a week.

C

CAR RENTAL/HIRE (See also Driving)

We don't recommend that you rent a car unless you plan to leave the city proper, since New York City has the highest car rental and parking rates in the US (as much as $80 per day). If you do need a car, though, you will find that it's generally cheaper to rent one at the airport than in Manhattan, and it's cheaper still to rent a car outside of New York City, where prices are more competitive. We strongly recommend that you make your reservation for car rental before you leave home.

You will need a major credit card to rent a car. The minimum age for renting a car is 21, but some companies will not rent to drivers under-25, or when they do will impose a high additional fee. Rental from JFK is approximately $60-$100/day. You will probably end up paying more in parking fees than rental costs.

Avis (www.avis.com) 800-633 3469
Budget (www.budget.com) 800-218 7992
Enterprise (www.enterprise.com) 844-362 0812
Hertz (www.hertz.com) 800-654 3131

CLIMATE

New York is a city of extremes when it comes to weather. Summers (mid-June to early September) in New York are hot and humid; winters (mid-November to late March) are generally cold. Spring (early April to mid-June) and fall (mid-September to mid-November) have the best weather. While the average low temperature in January is around -4°C, it can be as low as -15°C. The wind is a major factor in how cold it feels when you are walking in the city. In summer it can get very humid with extremes at close to 38°C.

CLOTHING

Casual dress is fine for most places in New York, including restaurants and theaters. Only a very few restaurants strictly enforce jacket and tie policies. In the summer, light clothing made of natural fibers is recommended because of the heat and humidity. In winter, hats and gloves will go a long way to keeping the wind and cold at bay. Make sure to bring layers to cope with both the very cold and more moderate days.

CRIME AND SAFETY (See also Emergencies)

While New York is the safest major city in the US, petty theft is still common, especially pick-pocketing at crowded intersections and subway train entrances. If you are robbed, report it to the police (tel: 646-610 5000 or 311 for non-emergencies; 911 for emergencies): your insurance company will need to see a copy of the police report (as may your consulate if your passport is stolen).

CUSTOMS REGULATIONS

You can bring into the US the following duty free items: one liter of alcohol, if over 21 years of age; 200 cigarettes, 50 cigars, or 2kg of tobacco, if you are over 18; and gifts worth up to $100 ($800 for US citizens. Travelers with more than $10,000 in US or foreign currency, traveler's checks, or money orders must declare these upon entry. Meats, fruits, vegetables, seeds, or plants (and, note, even sealed prepared foods from them) are not permitted and must be disposed in the receptacles provided before entering. For more information, contact US Customs and Border Protection (tel: 877-227 5511; "Know Before You Go" document on www.cbp.gov).

D

DRIVING (See also Car rental/hire)

Driving conditions. Visitors arriving by car would do well to leave their vehicle parked in a garage and use public transportation, as traffic and scarce parking space make driving a nightmare. If you must drive, remember the following rules: the speed limit is 30mph (50kmh) unless otherwise indicated; you may not (legally) use your horn in the city; the use of seat belts is mandatory; the speed limit on most highways in the city is 55mph (90kmh) and strictly enforced – look for signs, as on some major highways it has been raised to 65mph (105kmh); right-hand turns are prohibited at all red lights in the city; and, of course, visitors must remember to drive on the right. Before leaving home, determine whether your own insurance will cover you when you are driving a rented car.

Parking. While street parking is possible in some areas outside of Midtown, a garage or parking lot is the safer though far more expensive choice (www.nyc.bestparking.com and www.iconparkingsystems.com are useful for locating parking garages at discounted rates). If you find a parking spot, obey parking regulations, which may include parking only on one side of the street on alternate days (call 311 for more information). Never park next to a fire hydrant and don't leave your car over the time limit, or it may be towed away.

Gas (petrol). Service stations are scarce in the city (Eleventh and Twelfth avenues on the West Side are good hunting grounds).

Breakdowns and insurance. AAA Northeast (https://northeast.aaa.

com), a branch of the American Automobile Association (AAA), will help members as well as foreign visitors affiliated with other recognized automobile associations. In case of a breakdown, or for other problems along the way, call their Emergency Road Service (tel: 800-222 4357) or wait until a police car comes along.

AAA New York: 1140 Franklin Avenue, Garden City, NY 11530, tel: 516-873 2382; https://northeast.aaa.com.

E

ELECTRICITY

110-volt 60-cycle AC is standard throughout the US. Plugs are the flat, parallel two-pronged variety. Foreign visitors without dual-voltage appliances will need a transformer and adapter plug.

EMBASSIES AND CONSULATES

Embassies are located in Washington, DC, but most countries have consulates or missions to the United Nations in New York.

Australia: Consulate General, 150 East 42nd Street, tel: 212-351 6500; www.newyork.consulate.gov.au

Canada: 1251 Avenue of the Americas, tel: 212-596 1628; http://international.gc.ca

Ireland: 345 Park Avenue, tel: 212-319 2555; www.dfa.ie/irish-consulate/newyork

New Zealand Mission to the UN: 600 Third Avenue, tel: 212-826 1960; www.mfat.govt.nz

South Africa: 333 E. 38th Street, tel: 212-213 4880; www.southafrica-newyork.net

UK: 845 Third Avenue, tel: 212-745 0200; www.gov.uk/government/world/organisations/british-consulate-general-new-york

EMERGENCIES (See also Health and medical care and Police)

All-purpose emergency number: 911

G

GETTING THERE

By air. Most airlines have several flights a day to one of New York's airports. Newark is a hub for United Airlines; from Europe it is served by British Airways, Austrian Airlines, Lufthansa, Scandinavian Airlines and Virgin Atlantic; and from Canada by Air Canada. Other airlines with flights into Newark include American and Delta; many have international connections. JFK is a hub for Air France, American, British Airways and Virgin Atlantic; connections to any European airline are good, as are connections to Canada, and to Asia and the Pacific via Cathay Pacific. LaGuardia, which serves mostly domestic flights, is a hub of Delta and American; United also uses LaGuardia, as does Air Canada.

GUIDES AND TOURS

A good way to get started in New York is to take advantage of one of the double-decker hop-on-hop-off bus tours. For those visitors who don't want to deal with New York's transit system on their own, these are an ideal option. One choice is **Gray Line** (terminal at 777 Eighth Avenue between 47th and 48th streets, tel: 212-445 0848; www.newyorksightseeing.com).

Numerous companies offer a variety of themed tours. Cyclists should contact **Central Park Bicycle Tours**, tel: 212-541 8759; https://centralparkbiketours.com. Go in search of Edgar Allan Poe and his ghostly friends in a walking tour of East Village with **Ghosts of New York** (tel: 646-844 4578; www.ghostsofny.com). **Harlem Heritage Tours** (104 Malcolm X Boulevard, tel: 212-280 7888; www.harlemheritage.com) provides an insider's view of Harlem, and with **Harlem Spirituals** (690 Eighth Avenue, tel: 212-391 0900; www.harlemspirituals.com) you can join jazz and gospel tours. The **Municipal Art Society of New York** (488 Madison Avenue, tel: 212-935 3960; www.mas.org) puts on history and architecture tours, while nature tours in city parks can be undertaken with **Urban Park** Rangers (tel: 311 or 212-360 2768; www.nycgovparks.

org/programs/rangers; for Central Park tours, tel: 212-310 6600; www.
centralparknyc.org). Finally, there is **Big Onion Walking Tours** (476 13th
Street, tel: 888-606 9255 or 212-439 1090; www.bigonion.com) for tours
downtown.

H

HEALTH AND MEDICAL CARE

New York has many of the country's top hospitals. Payment for any
medical services will be billed in full, and the bill will probably be ex-
orbitantly high. Arrange for health insurance before your visit. In an
emergency, your hotel should be able to provide a list of doctors. Tap
water is perfectly safe in New York.

Pharmacies. There are many pharmacies in New York that are open 24
hours including the following:

CVS, 150 East 42nd Street, tel: 212-661 8139

CVS, 630 Lexington Avenue at 53rd Street, tel: 917-369 8688

Walgreen's, 145 Fourth Avenue (at 14th Street), tel: 212-677 0214; www.
walgreens.com

L

LGBTQ TRAVELERS

New York has a sizable LGBTQ population. While Greenwich Village, especially Christopher Street, is still a center for gay life, Chelsea is now
the more fashionable gay neighborhood, where many gay restaurants
and shops can be found (especially along Eighth Avenue from 14th to
23rd streets). For gay events and nightlife information, see *Time Out
New York* or *The Village Voice* (www.villagevoice.com). Publications include *Gay City News* (www.gaycitynews.com), covering local, national
and international news. Gay and Lesbian Hotline tel: 212-989 0999.
Lesbian, Gay, Bisexual and Transgender Community Center tel. 212-
620 7310; www.gaycenter.org.

LOST PROPERTY

Each transport system maintains its own lost property office. Here are two useful numbers: **New York City Transit Authority** (nycta, subway network and bus system) Lost Property Office: tel: 212-712 4500 or 511; http://lostfound.mtanyct.info and NYC **Taxi and Limousine Commission Lost Property:** tel: 311.

M

MAPS

Most hotels offer free maps but you can also pick them up at Official NYC Information centers and kiosks.

MEDIA

Magazines and newspapers. The city's major daily newspapers are the *Daily News, New York Times,* and *New York Post.* Several local weeklies, including *The New Yorker, New York Magazine,* and *Time Out New York* have information about goings on about town. *The Village Voice,* also weekly, is an online only publication (www.village voice.com).

Radio and television. Channel 1 (NY1) on Time-Warner cable systems is a 24-hour station devoted to local news, weather, and events. There are about 50 local AM and FM radio stations in the New York area, including 1010 WINS (AM) for traffic, news, and weather.

MONEY

Currency. There are 100 cents in the dollar. The coins are: 1¢ (penny), 5¢ (nickel), 10¢ (dime), 25¢ (quarter), and $1. Bank notes of $1, $5, $10, $20, $50, and $100 are common, but some places will not accept denominations over $20 unless you make a large purchase.

Exchange. Branches of the Chase Manhattan Bank, Citibank, and the bigger offices of other major banks change foreign currency. You can also exchange money at People's Foreign Exchange (60 East

42nd Street, Lobby #16, across from Grand Central Station; www. peoplesfx.com), which is open weekdays 9am–6pm and weekends 10am–4pm.

Traveler's checks. If you prefer to carry traveler's checks, buy them in US$. Foreign currency traveler's checks must be exchanged at a bank.

ATMs. Most banks charge a small fee to non-depositors to use their atm machines.

O

OPENING HOURS

Banks: Mon–Fri 9am–3 or 4pm; many open Sat 9am–2pm. Some banks, such as TD Bank, are now offering longer opening hours (7.30am–8pm) and Sunday openings (11am–4pm).

Offices: 9am–5pm is the norm.

Stores: Mon–Sat 10am–6pm; some open until 7 or 8pm and most on Sun noon–6pm.

Restaurants: Most are open until at least 11pm during the week, and until midnight or later on Friday and Saturday. Some are closed on Mondays.

P

POLICE (See also Crime and Emergencies)

In an emergency, dial 911.

POST OFFICES

Post offices are generally open weekdays 8am–5pm and on Saturday 9am–1pm. New York's General Post Office (421 Eighth Avenue, New York, NY 10001; www.usps.com) has extended hours (Mon–Fri 7am–10pm, Sat 9am–9pm, Sun 11am–7pm). You can buy stamps at hotel reception desks, in many grocery stores, or from stamp machines. Mailboxes are painted blue.

PUBLIC HOLIDAYS

The following are national holidays in the US. In New York City, banks, offices, and some stores and museums are closed on these days:

New Year's Day January 1
Martin Luther King, Jr. Day Third Monday in January
President's Day Third Monday in February
Memorial Day Last Monday in May
Independence Day July 4
Labor Day First Monday in September
Columbus Day Second Monday in October
Veterans' Day November 11
Thanksgiving Day Fourth Thursday in November
Christmas Day December 25

T

TELEPHONES

Public pay phones are scarce in New York; you are better off buying a pre-paid cell phone SIM. In order to use a US SIM card you need to ensure your phone is both unlocked and quad band. If so, you can purchase a card from any mobile phone store (which are numerous: AT&T, T-Mobile, Verizon, and others). However, this will not be a cheap option for international calls, so you may want to use pre-paid phone cards to call from a landline instead.

The country code for the US is 1 and should be dialed before any area code when using a landline. New York has five area codes: 212 and 646 for Manhattan; 917 mainly for cell phones, but also for Manhattan; 718 and 347 for the Bronx, Queens, Brooklyn, and Staten Island. Area codes are followed by a seven digit number. For international calls, dial 011 + the country code + the number. Newsstands and drug stores sell calling cards for long-distance calls.

All numbers with an 800, 888, or 877 prefix are toll-free. You can dial directory assistance (411) for free from any phone.

TIME ZONES

New York City is on Eastern Standard Time. In summer (between mid-March and early November), Daylight Saving Time is adopted, and clocks move ahead one hour. The time in various cities in winter:

Los Angeles	**New York**	London	Paris	Sydney
9am	noon	**5pm**	6pm	4am

TIPPING

Service is never included in restaurant prices, but it is sometimes added to the bill when you are a group of six or more. In restaurants and bars, tip 15–20 percent of the total bill (New Yorkers traditionally double the sales tax). In general, porters are tipped $1–2 per bag; maids $1–2 per day; cloakroom attendants and doormen who find you a taxi, $1; taxi drivers and hairdressers, 15–20 percent.

TOILETS

Clean public toilets are hard to come by in Manhattan. In general, the best facilities are those in the lobbies of major hotels or in department stores. Good bets in the Times Square area are the Marriott Marquis, and the Times Square Visitor Center; in Lower Manhattan, the Museum of the American Indian, and World Financial Center. There are also public toilets in Washington Square Park (closed at night).

TOURIST INFORMATION

There are three NYC (www.nycgo.com) Official Information Centers in New York City: at **Times Square** (TKTS Plaza, Broadway at 47th Street; daily 8am–7pm); **Macy's Herald Square** (see page 67) (151 W. 34th Street, Mon–Sat 10am–10pm, Sun 10am–9pm) and **City Hall** (at the southern end of City Hall Park; daily 9am–6pm).

TRANSPORTATION (See also Airports)

Virtually every place that visitors are likely to go can be reached by public transportation. The basic fare is $2.75 (for bus or subway) one-way
when you buy a **MetroCard**. Single fare tickets (when bought from the
driver or vending machine) are $3. If you purchase a MetroCard, you
can transfer between buses and subways for free. In addition to paying
for each ride, you may buy an unlimited seven-day ($32) MetroCard.
MetroCards can be purchased at all subway stations and at many drug
and grocery stores and newsstands, including some supermarkets, and
will be subject to a $1 fee. Bus and subway maps are available at major
subway stations and transit hubs. For directions to reach any address in
New York City by public transportation, tel: 511. See also www.mta.info.

Buses. All public buses are numbered and for Manhattan bear the prefix M (Q for Queens, B for Brooklyn, and Bx for the Bronx). Most either
follow the avenues (except Park Avenue) or run cross-town along the
major two-way arteries. They only accept the exact fare, or a Metro-
Card. Bus stops are indicated by a signpost showing a blue-and-white
bus logo, and the bus number.

Subway. The network runs 24 hours a day, but not all entrances and
token booths are open at all times. You may wish to avoid peak times (7–
9.30am and 4.30–7pm). It is generally possible to make free transfers
from one line to another at major transfer points. Local trains make
every stop on the line; express trains do not. Lines are color-coded and
identified by the last station on the line. Ensure you know the direc-
tion you are traveling in: *downtown* is southwards, *uptown* northwards.
Despite occasional incidents, the subway is very safe: more than 5.5
million New Yorkers ride it every day, and on many lines in Manhattan,
you'll see as many people on the train at 2am as you will at 2pm.

Commuter rail lines. The Long Island Rail Road provides rail service
from Penn Station at 33rd Street and Seventh Avenue between Manhattan and Long Island (tel: 718-217 5477 or 511; www.mta.info/lirr). The
Metro-North commuter railroad provides rail service between Manhattan and counties to the north of New York, including southwest Con-

necticut (tel: 511; www.mta.info). PATH trains go from 33rd Street and Sixth Avenue or the World Financial Center to Hoboken, Jersey City, and Newark in New Jersey (fare is $2.75 using a Metrocard, tel: 800-234 7284; www.panynj.gov/path).

Taxis. Taxis are painted yellow and metered. If the light on top is lit, the cab is available. In Manhattan you can easily hail a taxi on the street, or go to a major hotel's taxi stand. Every taxi driver is expected to be able to speak English and to be able to take you to any address in New York City; they cannot legally refuse a fare if you are going to a destination within the city limits. The meter starts at $3.30 and increases by 50¢ every fifth of a mile (or 40¢ for waiting time). There is a 50¢ surcharge from 8pm–6am and a $1 surcharge for peak hours (4–8pm weekdays). If your route comprises a toll tunnel or bridge, you must pay the toll. Taxi drivers will not accept bills higher than $20 and they generally expect a tip (about 15–20 percent or round up to the nearest dollar). They now accept credit cards for all fares. To complain about a driver, note his or her name and number and call 311. Such complaints are taken seriously.

TRAVELERS WITH DISABILITIES

Most New York street corners are graded for wheelchairs. Buses can accommodate wheelchairs, though many subway stations are not accessible. Many hotels have rooms for guests with disabilities, but check when you make your reservation because some older establishments do not. The Mayor's Office for People with Disabilities (100 Gold Street, 2nd Floor, New York, NY 10038, tel: 311; www1.nyc.gov/site/mopd/index.page) can provide further details.

V

VISAS AND ENTRY REQUIREMENTS (See also Airports)

Canadians traveling by air must present a valid passport for entry. Visitors from the UK, Australia, New Zealand, and Ireland qualify for the visa waiver program, and therefore do not need a visa for stays of less than 90 days, as long as they have a valid 10-year machine-readable passport and a return ticket. However, they must apply online for authorization at least 72 hours before traveling at https://esta.cbp.dhs.gov/esta. Citizens of South Africa need a visa. All foreign visitors have their two index fingers scanned and a digital photograph taken at the port of entry. The process takes only 10–15 seconds.

W

WEBSITES

The following websites will help you plan your trip:
www.citysearch.com/guide/newyork-ny-metro CitySearch
www.nycgo.com Official NYC Information Center
www.timeout.com/newyork events, bar and restaurant listings
www.mta.info regional transportation options
www1.nyc.gov New York City Government's website
http://ny.eater.com reviews of the city's restaurants and eateries.

WEIGHTS AND MEASURES

The United States uses the Imperial system.

Y

YOUTH HOSTELS AND YMCAS [See also Accommodations]

The Hostelling International New York City Hostel is located at 891 Amsterdam Avenue, NYC 10025 (tel: 212-932 2300; www.hihostels.com). There are also two YMCA where you can have a single or shared room with access to shared baths on a sex-segregated floor with exercise facilities: the Vanderbilt YMCA, 224 East 47th Street, NYC 10017 (tel: 212-912 2500); and the West Side YMCA, 5 West 63rd Street, NYC 10023 (tel: 212-912 2600; www.ymcanyc.org). There are also YMCAs in Harlem, Flushing and Greenpoint (see website for details).

RECOMMENDED HOTELS

The only way to beat New York's notoriously high hotel rates is to come during the off-season (roughly Jan–Mar) or to get a package deal or weekend special. Advance reservations are essential most of the year. You will find the highest concentration of hotels in Midtown, between 42nd and 59th streets; others are in the 30s, both on the west side (near Herald Square) and on the east side (Murray Hill, including Gramercy Park). What you will not find here are most of the $500-plus luxury hotels.

Inquire direct about weekend specials; otherwise use one of the many online reservation services offering discounts of 50 percent or more on upscale rooms (www.kayak.com, www.hotels.com and www.priceline.com, to name a few).

The following categories apply to the cost of a standard or superior double room for one night and do not include tax of 14.75 percent plus $3.50 per night occupancy tax or the additional $25 per night changed by hotels located close to Times Square. Unless otherwise indicated, rooms have private baths, direct-dial phones, cable television, and air-conditioning.

$$$$$	over $500
$$$$	$400–500
$$$	$300–400
$$	$200–300
$	below $200

DOWNTOWN

Mercer Hotel $$$$ *147 Mercer Street, NYC 10012, tel: 212-966 6060;* www.mercerhotel.com. A converted 1890s landmark building right in the heart of SoHo, the rooms feature high loft ceilings, arched windows, and (for New York) spacious bath facilities. Expect a stylish clientele and great food from the acclaimed Mercer Kitchen restaurant. 75 rooms.

Mr. C Seaport $$$ *33 Peck Slip, NYC 10038, tel: 877-528 4249*; www.mrc-seaport.com. A block from South Street Seaport, this converted 19th-century warehouse features contemporary, Italian style rooms with all modern amenities. Children are well catered for with homemade cookies and milk provided on their first night. Some rooms on the upper floors have private terraces with views of the Brooklyn Bridge. 66 rooms.

Soho Grand Hotel $$$ *310 West Broadway, NYC 10013, tel: 212-965 3000*; www.sohogrand.com. A sophisticated but comfortable hotel with all the high-tech and stylish amenities you might expect from an upscale hostelry that caters to the media and music-biz crowds. As befits a place owned by the heir to the Hartz Mountain pet empire, pets are welcome; for anyone who arrives without an animal companion, the management may be able to provide a complimentary bowl of goldfish. 353 rooms and suites.

Washington Square Hotel $$ *103 Waverly Place (MacDougal Street and 6th Avenue), NYC 10011, tel: 212-777 9515*; www.washingtonsquarehotel.com. This small, century-old, Art Deco hotel in Greenwich Village is one of the very few inexpensive options available downtown. Guest rooms, some of which look out over the park, are brightly decorated, and the restaurant, North Square, is one of the neighborhood's hidden secrets. 149 rooms.

MIDTOWN

The Benjamin $$$ *125 East 50th Street (at Lexington Avenue), NYC 10022, tel: 212-715 2500 or 1866-222 2365*; www.thebenjamin.com. One of New York City's boutique-style hotels, the Benjamin offers business and leisure travelers four-star amenities and some of the most comfortable beds in New York, at relatively reasonable prices. Rooms have galley kitchens with a microwave and fridge, and some have terraces. There is also a spa, fitness center, restaurant, and cocktail lounge. The lovely Art Deco building was erected in 1927, the work of world-renowned architect Emery Roth. 209 rooms.

Casablanca Hotel $$$$ *147 West 43rd Street (6th Avenue and Broadway), NYC 10036, tel: 212-869 1212*; www.casablancahotel.com. Wonderful, small hotels are rare in New York, yet here is a lovely and inviting choice. The décor throughout evokes Morocco, with Murano glass hallway sconces and beautifully tiled and appointed bathrooms. Continental breakfast included. 48 rooms.

Hotel Edison $$$ *228 West 47th Street (Broadway and 8th Avenue), NYC 10036, tel: 212-840 5000; www.edisonhotelnyc.com.* Though the Art Deco lobby can be chaotic, the rooms in this huge hotel are quite comfortable, pleasantly if simply decorated, and quiet. There is a large fitness center available. The complimentary walking tours are a good opportunity to learn about the neighbourhood. May be the best deal in NYC. 802 rooms.

Four Seasons Hotel New York $$$$$ *57 East 57th Street (Park and Madison avenues), NYC 10022, tel: 212-758 5700; www.fourseasons.com.* Arguably New York's best hotel, the Four Seasons has some of the largest rooms in the city (along with some of the highest prices). Elegant features include blond wood furnishings, bedside controls for everything, and separate showers and tubs. The lobby bar is also top-notch. 368 rooms.

Hotel Iroquois $$$$ *49 West 44th Street (5th and 6th avenues), NYC 10036, tel: 212-840 3080 or 800-332-7220; www.iroquoisny.com.* This luxurious boutique hotel is close enough to the theater district to be convenient, but far enough away to be out of the path of most of the crowds. Standard rooms are not large, but they accommodate a king-size bed without feeling too cramped. The health club is first-rate. 114 rooms.

Mandarin Oriental $$$$$ *80 Columbus Circle, NYC 10023, tel: 212-805 8800; www.mandarinoriental.com.* Offering suites with beautiful views over Central Park and the rest of Manhattan, this five star hotel provides not only a stunning setting, but also top of the notch service, comfort and style. There is also a spa, pool, glamorous cocktail bar, and celebrated restaurant. 248 rooms and suites.

Mansfield $$$ *12 West 44th Street (5th and 6th avenues), NYC 10036, tel: 212-277 8700 or 844-591 5565; www.mansfieldhotel.com.* A carefully restored Edwardian gem, the Mansfield is situated off the crush of Times Square. The only drawback is that standard rooms are small and lack real closets. Suites, however, are sumptuous. 126 rooms.

Millennium Broadway $$$ *145 West 44th Street (6th Avenue and Broadway), NYC 10036, tel: 212-768 4400*; www.millenniumhotels.com. All of the rooms in this modern neoclassic tower are large and tastefully appointed, and all feature the usual business hotel amenities. 626 rooms and suites.

Paramount Hotel $$$–$$$$ *235 West 46th Street (8th Avenue and Broadway), NYC 10036, tel: 212-764 5500 or 844-881 5314*; www.nycparamount.com. A mix of retro and contemporary in the heart of Times Square. The rooms and public spaces pay homage to the theater design of the 1920s, but through a modern and minimalist lens. Amenities include extravagant 'entertainment suites,' access to the hotel's iPads and iMacs, and a classic theater district bar. Rooms are small but well equipped. 605 rooms.

Pod 51 Hotel $$ *230 East 51st Street, NYC 10022, tel: 212-355 0300*; www.thepodhotel.com. This hotel will appeal to visitors on a budget looking for style and a dock for their iPhone. Rooms with bunk beds start at under $100 per night in low season. Rooms with a shared bath have in-room displays to indicate the availability of shared bathrooms. 348 rooms, including some with shared bath.

The Roosevelt $$$ *Madison Avenue (at 45th Street), NYC 10017, tel. 212 661 9600*; www.theroosevelthotel.com. This large hotel near Grand Central Terminal has been renovated. Rooms are traditionally decorated. Popular with tour groups, it is a good base from which to explore the city if you don't want to be in the Times Square area. 1,025 rooms.

Sanctuary Hotel $$$ *132 West 47th Street (6th and 7th avenues), NYC 10036, tel: 212-234 7000 or 800-388 8988*; www.sanctuaryhotelnyc.com. Prices are reasonable, the style is hip and modern, and theater lovers will find the location ideal. 113 rooms.

The Shoreham $$$$ *33 West 55th Street (5th and 6th avenues), NYC 10019, tel: 855-212 6773*; www.shorehamhotel.com. On a quiet residential street just around the corner from the Museum of Modern Art, this boutique hotel has a sleek, stylish lobby and bar. Rooms are fairly small but sumptuous and comfortable. 177 rooms.

St Regis $$$$$ *2 East 55th Street (at 5th Avenue), NYC 10022, tel: 212-753 4500;* www.starwoodhotels.com. Among the best of New York's palatial hotels, the St Regis is in the sweet spot of Fifth Avenue, right around the corner from MoMA and the most glittering shops. The Beaux Arts design is authentic from 1904. Rooms contrast high-tech amenities with French antiques; the King Cole Bar is famed for its Maxfield Parrish murals. 238 rooms.

HERALD SQUARE, MURRAY HILL, GRAMERCY PARK

Ace Hotel $$$$ *20 West 29th Street (at Broadway), NYC 10001, tel: 212-679 2222 or 212-991 0551;* www.acehotel.com/newyork. The hotel boasts a hip clientele, a celebrated restaurant and stylish rooms. At night, the lobby transforms into a club.

Affinia Shelburne $$$ *303 Lexington Avenue (at 37th Street), NYC 10016, tel: 212-689 5200;* www.affinia.com. With an eclectic, contemporary decor, the Shelburne, a member of the Affinia group, offers good-sized suites some with stunning views. Many suites have modern sleek kitchenettes and sofabeds. A good choice for families and business travelers. Order a room service hamburger from Rare Bar and Grill downstairs. Fitness center. 325 rooms. Other Affinia hotels in New York include Fifty Hotel (155 East 50th Street, tel: 212-751 5710) with a newly renovated fitness center.

Deauville Hotel $$ *103 East 29th Street (Park and Lexington avenues), NYC 10016, tel: 212-683 0990 or 800-333 8843;* www.hoteldeauville.com. This inexpensive hotel is popular with budget travelers (small rooms with shared bath can go for under $100), but it is a good location for anyone looking for a clean and simple room. The friendly staff will make you feel right at home. 54 rooms.

The Evelyn $$$ *7 East 27th Street (5th and Madison avenues), NYC 10016, tel: 212-545 8000;* www.theevelyn.com. A stylish boutique hotel in a red brick building right next to Madison Square Park. Rooms are beautifully decorated, with contemporary furnishings and wood floors have some luxurious touches. 160 rooms.

The Hotel @ New York City $$$ *161 Lexington Avenue (at 30th Street), NYC 10016, tel: 212-545 1800;* www.applecorehotels.com. A lovely, small Murray Hill boutique hotel. It has a 24-hour fitness center and good restaurants nearby on Lexington Avenue. Continental breakfast included. 111 rooms.

Life Hotel $$$ *19 West 31st Street (5th Avenue and Broadway), NYC 10001, tel: 212-615 9900;* www.lifehotel.com. The former headquarters of *Life* magazine is now a swanky hotel which mixes the old architecture with modern decoration. The hotel boasts a good restaurant, Henry at Life Hotel. 98 rooms and suites.

Hotel Metro $$$ *45 West 35th Street (5th and 6th avenues), NYC 10001, tel: 212-947 2500;* www.hotelmetronyc.com. The lovely Art Deco lobby, with fresh flowers and leather chairs, is an oasis from gritty 35th Street. Guest rooms are fairly large and meticulously clean; the family suites are a good choice, offering two separate sleeping areas for less than the price of two rooms. Great value. 183 rooms and suites.

The Roger $$$$$ *131 Madison Avenue (at 31st Street), NYC 10016, tel: 212-448 7000 or 877-670 1617;* www.therogernewyork.com. This boutique hotel near Madison Square Park and the Flatiron Building, with a soaring lobby and soothing rooms, appeals to travelers who look for style with their room. The well-sized guest rooms make for a relaxing stay and an attractive choice in Murray Hill. Many rooms offer views of the Empire State Building. Continental breakfast included. 194 rooms.

St Giles: The Tuscany $$$ *120 East 39th Street, NYC 10016, tel: 212-686 1600;* www.stgileshotels.com. This luxury boutique hotel is part of the St Giles chain of high-tech, upscale business hotels. The large rooms have all the trimmings you would expect at these prices, including free Wi-Fi, dataports and dual-line phones. 124 rooms and suites.

Hotel Wolcott $$$ *4 West 31st Street (5th Avenue and Broadway), NYC 10001, tel: 212-268 2900;* www.wolcott.com. The gilded lobby in this reasonably priced hotel is an attractive holdover from the Edith Wharton age. A standout in its price category. Rooms come with one, two, or three beds and are well-kept and clean. Small fitness center. 200 rooms.

THE UPPER EAST SIDE

The Franklin $$$ *164 East 87th Street (3rd and Lexington avenues), NYC 10128, tel: 212-369 1000 or 800-607 4009; www.franklinhotel.com.* The old-fashioned exterior of the Franklin doesn't prepare you for the elegant and stylish modern rooms inside. Though not large, all the modern details have been well thought out, and the human scale of the place and the hotel's friendly staff are definite pluses. Convenient to the subway and Fifth Avenue museums. 50 rooms.

Hotel Wales $$$ *1295 Madison Avenue (near 92nd Street) NYC 10128, tel: 212-876 6000 or 866-925 3746; www.hotelwalesnyc.com.* The oldest operating hotel in New York is ideally situated for visiting museums on Museum Mile. The rooftop terrace offers views of the Central Park reservoir. Rooms are elegantly furnished with great attention to detail. Room service is offered from Sarabeth's (see page 113). 87 rooms.

THE UPPER WEST SIDE

Hotel Beacon $$ *2130 Broadway (at 75th Street), NYC 10023, tel: 212-787 1100 or 800-572 4949; www.beaconhotel.com.* An apartment building converted into a hotel. The good news for travelers is that a cramped New York apartment makes a spacious hotel room, and every room has either a king bed or two double beds and fully equipped kitchenettes. Convenient for the Beacon Theater, Lincoln Center, Natural History Museum, and Central Park. More than 270 rooms.

Lucerne Hotel $$$ *201 West 79th Street, NYC 10024, tel: 212-875 1000 or 800-492 8122; www.thelucernehotel.com.* Housed in the beautifully renovated 1904 building, this boutique hotel boasts elegantly furnished comfortable rooms. Some suites include kitchenettes. Spa services, 24-hour room service, and fitness center are available as well as the restaurant, Nice Matin. 202 rooms and suites.

INDEX

INSIGHT ⊙ GUIDES POCKET GUIDE

NEW YORK

Second Edition 2019

Editor: Sian Marsh
Author: Douglas Stallings
Head of DTP and Pre-Press: Rebeka Davies
Picture Editor: Tom Smyth
Cartography Update: Carte
Update Production: Apa Digital
Photography Credits: Abe Nowitz/Apa Publications 4TC, 39, 55, 60, 61, 65, 67, 76, 78; Anna Mockford & Nick Bonetti/Apa Publications 5TC, 47; AWL Images 1; Britta Jaschinski/Apa Publications 4MC, 4ML, 26, 29, 30, 40, 42, 43, 44, 48, 52, 57, 59, 87, 89, 91, 94, 97; Getty Images 12, 17; iStock 7, 18, 25, 35, 46, 62, 74, 80, 83, 84, 92, 101, 103, 104; Keiko Niwa/Lower East Side Tenement Museum 71; Marley White/NYC & Co 11; Michael Bodycomb/The Frick Collection 51; Public domain 14, 53; Richard Nowitz/Apa Publications 41L, 33, 36, 72, 73, 106; Shutterstock 5T, 5MC, 5M, 5MC, 5M, 6L, 6R, 7R, 41, 81; Tagger Yancey IV/NYC & Company 22; The Metropolitan Museum of Art 69
Cover Picture: iStock

Distribution
UK, Ireland and Europe: Apa Publications (UK) Ltd; sales@insightguides.com
United States and Canada: Ingram Publisher Services; ips@ingramcontent.com
Australia and New Zealand: Woodslane; info@woodslane.com.au
Southeast Asia: Apa Publications (SN) Pte; singaporeoffice@insightguides.com
Worldwide: Apa Publications (UK) Ltd; sales@insightguides.com

Special Sales, Content Licensing and CoPublishing
Insight Guides can be purchased in bulk quantities at discounted prices. We can create special editions, personalised jackets and corporate imprints tailored to your needs. sales@insightguides.com; www.insightguides.biz

Contact us
Every effort has been made to provide accurate information in this publication, but changes are inevitable. The publisher cannot be responsible for any resulting loss, inconvenience or injury. We would appreciate it if readers would call our attention to any errors or outdated information. We also welcome your suggestions; please contact us at: hello@insightguides.com
www.insightguides.com

INSIGHT ⊙ GUIDES
OFF THE SHELF

Since 1970, **INSIGHT GUIDES** has provided a unique perspective on the world's best travel destinations by using specially commissioned photography and illuminating text written by local authors.

Whether you're planning a city break, a walking tour or the journey of a lifetime, our superb range of guidebooks and phrasebooks will inspire you to discover more about your chosen destination.

INSIGHT GUIDES
offer a unique combination of stunning photos, absorbing narrative and detailed maps, providing all the inspiration and information you need.

PHRASEBOOKS & DICTIONARIES
help users to feel at home, when away. Pocket-sized with a free app to download, they go where you do.

CITY GUIDES
pack hundreds of great photos into a smaller format with detailed practical information, so you can navigate the world's top cities with confidence.

EXPLORE GUIDES
feature easy-to-follow walks and itineraries in the world's most exciting destinations, with our choice of the best places to eat and drink along the way.

POCKET GUIDES
combine concise information on where to go and what to do in a handy compact format, ideal on the ground. Includes a full-colour, fold-out map.

EXPERIENCE GUIDES
feature offbeat perspectives and secret gems for experienced travellers, with a collection of over 100 ideas for a memorable stay in a city.

www.insightguides.com